A LETTER TO MY ANXIOUS CHRISTIAN FRIENDS

From Fear to Faith in Unsettled Times

DAVID P. GUSHEE

WESTMINSTER
JOHN KNOX PRESS
LOUISVILLE · KENTUCKY

© 2016 David P. Gushee

First edition
Published by Westminster John Knox Press
Louisville, Kentucky

16 17 18 19 20 21 22 23 24 25—10 9 8 7 6 5 4 3 2 1

Scripture quotations are from the New Revised Standard Version of the Bible, copyright © 1989 by the Division of Christian Education of the National Council of the Churches of Christ in the U.S.A., and are used by permission.

Book design by Erika Lundbom-Krift
Cover design by Mary Ann Smith
Cover illustration and photo: Mary Ann Smith

Library of Congress Cataloging-in-Publication Data

Names: Gushee, David P., 1962- author.
Title: A letter to my anxious Christian friends : from fear to faith in unsettled times / David P. Gushee.
Description: Louisville, KY : Westminster John Knox Press, 2016.
Identifiers: LCCN 2016011999 (print) | LCCN 2016015674 (ebook) | ISBN 9780664262686 (alk. paper) | ISBN 9781611646948 (ebk.)
Subjects: LCSH: United States—Church history—21st century. | United States—Social conditions—21st century | Christians—Political activity—United States. | Trust in God—Christianity.
Classification: LCC BR526 .G87 2016 (print) | LCC BR526 (ebook) | DDC 277.3/083—dc23
LC record available at https://lccn.loc.gov/2016011999

PRINTED IN THE UNITED STATES OF AMERICA

♾ The paper used in this publication meets the minimum requirements of the American National Standard for Information Sciences—Permanence of Paper for Printed Library Materials, ANSI Z39.48-1992.

Most Westminster John Knox Press books are available at special quantity discounts when purchased in bulk by corporations, organizations, and special-interest groups. For more information, please e-mail SpecialSales@wjkbooks.com.

To every Christian who tries to love America

CONTENTS

INTRODUCTION

MY DEAR FELLOW AMERICAN CHRISTIANS: I WOULD LIKE to write you a letter about our country and how Christians should think about it and live in it right now. My main goal is to help American Christians to see our reality more clearly, assess that reality more thoughtfully, and act more faithfully. Are you interested in this? I hope so.

There is little question that Americans as a whole are anxious, with economic, cultural, and security anxieties at the top of the list for many of us. While the nation has by some measures recovered from the Great Recession of 2007–2008, many Americans have never really made it back to prosperity or just breaking even. Our cultural differences over all kinds of issues, such as race and sex, are like a scab that keeps getting torn off.

And we are more scared than we have ever been that if we go to a mall or a movie theater, someone is going to try to kill us.

Americans who claim a Christian identity share many of the same anxieties as everyone else but often have distinctive concerns. Our country is becoming more religiously diverse. Fewer people claim Christian identity, and the nation as a whole seems less culturally and publicly "Christian" than ever. A great many of our churches are struggling. Lifetime churchgoers often find that their children and grandchildren aren't interested in the faith. And cultural conflicts never just remain "out there"; often they migrate "in here" to our congregations and even our dinner tables.

In this book, I offer a series of brief, understandable reflections on some of the major anxiety-causing issues that we face together. In a context of vicious partisan fighting, I will do my best to offer peaceable, constructive ideas that can make sense to Christians who identify very differently in their politics. I hope to inject a note of realistic and empowering hope into a cultural and Christian climate filled with pessimism. That might be kind of nice, don't you think?

This book reflects a lifetime of working at the intersection of faith and politics, but I will not bore you with the footnotes or fancy words to prove it. Think of what follows as a letter from me to you, or twenty little letters, or maybe just us sitting over coffee and hashing a few things out as fellow Christians. There is a rough logic to the book's structure: the first eight chapters deal more with broad issues about American culture and democracy, while the remaining chapters tackle specific issue areas. But feel free to read the chapters in the order that interests you.

One final thought: the assumption lying behind this book is that it is okay for Christians to care enough about the country they live in to be anxious about it. It is, indeed, perfectly acceptable for Christians to be patriots, to love their country with a robust and full heart. Many of my fellow Christian leaders do not agree with me on this, and they have good reasons for their views. Mainly their worry is that American Christians, in particular, have a hard time distinguishing between God and country when they attempt to love and serve both. I think that I can point to a path of critical, informed patriotism through the various reflections offered here. But I acknowledge that I do love this country, and precisely because I do, I want it to be the best country it can be. If you agree, read on.

Chapter 1

AMERICA

Who Are We?

IT IS PRETTY MUCH IMPOSSIBLE TO WRAP OUR MINDS around this vast country called the United States of America. But here are a few forays, just for some perspective.

America is the third-most populous country in the world, with 320 million people. By land mass, we are the third- or fourth-largest country in the world. Stretching across an entire continent, with friendly neighbors to our north and south, geographically we are (were?) one of the most secure places on earth. We are also one of the most diverse in terms of geography and climate. The whole world, in a sense, is reflected on our soil. That's pretty cool.

Thinking of ourselves as one vast, continental, "sea to shining sea" country is, of course, quite natural. But it is helpful sometimes to think also of the United States in terms not so much of the fifty states (not to mention our territories and possessions) but of profoundly different local and regional cultures. These include, for example, the various contexts and life experiences of those who live in urban, suburban, exurban, and rural parts of America. These differences would occur in just about any country, or any similar country. Beyond this, however, think about the differences among our various regional cultures. Consider how different it is to live in the American South versus the Northeast. Then contrast both with the Northwest, and all the above with the Southwest and Midwest. And there's always the Republic of Texas. A lot of what baffles and divides us is regional. The idea that we are the "United" States of America sometimes feels fictional. One can easily imagine scenarios where this continent might have ended up with two, three, or even more separate countries if history had worked out differently. The Western States of America. The Duchy of New England. And so on.

By many measures of national strength, we have certainly gained numerous advantages by staying together. For example, we are uniquely favored with abundant and diverse natural resources across the length and breadth of our land, contributing to our tremendous economic power. We have developed a massive and productive economy that has remained strong in every era. Despite perceptions of American economic decline, and many individuals and families who struggle, as a nation we remain the single most powerful economic actor on the world stage and have the largest gross domestic product. We are a rich, innovative, economically productive and powerful country, even though we have an appalling number of people who are very poor.

The population of the United States began with native tribes who never recovered from the spread across the continent of European settlers and their own displacement and defeat in war. Surviving Native American tribes and individuals became America's most invisible people, and in some ways they remain our most troubled and impoverished population. It is striking how little attention Native Americans receive in contemporary U.S. politics and culture. Perhaps we would rather not think about it.

European settlers from many nations, though ultimately dominated by the British, and the African slaves they eventually brought here became the major early elements of the U.S. population. It must not be forgotten that Latin American (now often called Hispanic or Latino/a) people have been present in what became the United States ever since Spaniards reached Florida in the sixteenth century. Vastly more Latinos were incorporated into the U.S. population when the territory of the nation expanded to the west and southwest. Then successive waves of immigration over decades brought people from every nation to our own. For a long time, the United States has been one of the world's most ethnically diverse nations.

U.S. culture cannot be understood apart from thinking about the evolving layers of our population. Later we will return to the hot-button issue of immigration, but for now it is important to note that the powerful core founding population of settlers of European background (often called "white people," and there's much more to say about that) developed a deep sense of entitlement for controlling the politics and culture of what became the United States of America. This, tragically and unforgivably, included a sense of entitlement on the part of many to enslave persons from Africa and of African descent—and then to treat them as second-class noncitizens after they won their freedom from slavery. All these generations later, a much more diverse United States is experienced as threatening and unfamiliar by many of those who hail from European stock and still feel something of that sense of entitlement. Others excitedly wait and work toward a fully multicultural nation, with more people sharing in cultural, economic, and political power than ever before.

By any standard measure, the United States is one of the world's most stable countries. We have operated under the same democratic (federal, republican) system of government and the same constitution since 1789. That constitution, with its separation of powers, its checks and balances, and its shrewd understanding of human nature, became a model for other nations, many of whose people can still only dream of enjoying our level of political stability. Our founding political order has proven capable of serving a country larger and much more complex than the drafters could have imagined. The political design of our government and the civic culture that has helped sustain it over centuries are worthy of every American's respect and gratitude. But it is not merely an academic question to ask whether a sense of complacency about the impervious and enduring nature of our political system has tempted us to think that it can survive whatever abuses we actively inflict or passively permit.

I am among those who think that the wars of the twentieth century subtly affected our government and our culture while changing America's role in the world. We began as a loose group of colonies that, sufficiently outraged by British colonial injustices, banded together in the first successful anticolonial revolution of the modern era. We had, and still have, a great deal of "Don't tread on me" spirit in our national DNA. So it was certainly not inevitable that we would one day become a global superpower that would tread on a whole lot of other countries and peoples in the name of freedom or security.

But our smashing victories in World War I and World War II increased our confidence and global power. The Cold War left us as one of two global superpowers leading whole blocs of nations, everyone dangling over the nuclear-arms precipice and terrified of one another. The collapse of the USSR left us briefly as the world's only superpower, and we strutted a bit. Now the rise of radical Islamist terrorism has us terrified again.

The United States has become accustomed to vast global military, political, and economic power; to a massive and far-flung military and security apparatus; and to constant fighting around the world. This has strained our warriors and their families, as well as our constitutional order, because a constant state of emergency and war has never fit well with democratic governance.

As for religion, it is most fair to say that the colonies and then the United States began with a combination of personally devout and merely cultural Christianity, peculiarly mixed together with early Enlightenment religious skepticism and huge blind spots associated with slavery and race. All of this was characteristic of the situation of white European settlers in the era this continent was colonized. What has now become of this national religiosity is the topic of my next chapter.

The simple model I am working from in this open letter to you, my fellow American Christians, has three parts: see, assess, and act. I hope this brief reflection has helped you see a bit more clearly the grand epic that is the American story, an epic with much to celebrate but also much to mourn. I hope that sources of continued national strength are more visible now, and thus the current attitude of apparent national panic might be stilled a bit, at least in your heart. Ours is a great country, but like any country, it is a living, organic reality that changes over time. Some of those changes are constructive, some are dangerous, and some are subject to conflicting interpretations. Our actions and inactions as Christian citizens will be pivotal in affecting the direction that we now go as a nation.

Chapter 2

CHRISTIANS

Where Are We in This Country?

America was once a Christian nation.
America was never a Christian nation.

Which of these two statements rings true for you?
What rings true for me is this:

America was and was not a Christian nation.
And: America could never have been a Christian
nation, because there are no Christian nations.
And: Any nation that sanctioned slavery hardly mer-
its a designation as Christian.
However, America once saw itself as a Christian
nation—and doesn't so much anymore. That
is making a lot of today's American Christians
anxious and unhappy. And that anxiety and

unhappiness are affecting our politics, our culture, and a hundred different policy debates.

Let's try to analyze this complex problem. To speak in the broadest of terms, for the better part of two hundred years (and in the colonial era before that), the religious ecology of most parts of the United States of America was dominated by a culturally established Protestantism, with different kinds of Protestants taking the lead in different places. After many decades of being anti-Catholic, culturally established Protestantism finally broadened to include Catholicism on more-or-less equal terms. Culturally established Christianity stretched again to include Jews, leading to a broad "Judeo-Christian" religiosity by the late 1950s. Though the practice of Christianity, and one might add its devotional intensity, was stronger in some regions than in others, the public culture of the United States offered numerous signs of a broadly Christian, or Judeo-Christian, ethos. This ethos was strong enough that it is fair to say that ours was a "(Judeo-) Christian culture," if not a (Judeo-) Christian nation.

You could see that culture in a thousand different ways, though you would have to be of a certain age to remember it personally. (Or you have to have lived in a small Bible Belt town, as I did, where you can still see it to some extent even today.) It was visible in the mayor's prayer breakfast, with an invocation given by the local Episcopal priest or Baptist pastor. It was seen in the principal's recitation of the Lord's Prayer over the intercom at the start of the school day. It was obvious in the July 4 celebrations that mixed God and country, often seamlessly. It was noticeable in the way the court-house and the churches shared the same town squares, and the same people were often leaders in both. It was apparent in the way people would ask upon meeting each other, "Where do you go to church?" It was seen in the way Mom and Dad, Pastor Bob, Policeman Jim, Neighbor Lady Harriet, Dear Abby, and Aunt Mae all attempted to enforce the same broad moral code, now often called by the contested term "traditional values" but then just "right and wrong." Today it is seen mainly in nostalgic flashback, as in the vibe you get at a Cracker Barrel store or when watching *The Andy Griffith Show*.

There were certainly real limits on how much of this ethos was actually enshrined in law. The First Amendment banned the official establishment of any religion by the new federal government. Jesus was not a feature of the Constitution. But unlike in France, which was undergoing a bloody revolution at the same time, the official disestablishment of religion (aka Christianity) was not accompanied by an actively antireligious state policy or political culture. And there can be little question that a broadly Judeo-Christian moral code made its way into American law—for example, on such matters as marriage, abortion, and sexuality. Any honest reading of the historical forces leading to the First Amendment suggests that the goal was primarily to avoid intra-Christian sectarian conflict or injustice (e.g., state prosecution or persecution of Baptists by Episcopalians, of Quakers by Puritans, of skeptics by Christians), not to suppress the practice of Christianity. As Christianity flourished in an expanding United

States, American political culture made plenty of room for it, to say the least. What gradually coalesced and stabilized was an unofficial cultural Christianity that was expressed in a thousand different ways.

The period beginning in the 1960s brought a visible erosion of all these longstanding patterns. The cultural strength of Christianity began to weaken due to the rejection first of its moral values and then, more and more, of the religion as a whole. A gradual but relentlessly encroaching secularization has occurred, now claiming at least 20 percent of the American people.

But also, and perhaps just as important, left/right polarization, which has affected pretty much everything in American life and which I will address in another chapter, gradually began to affect Christianity deeply. (The same polarization happened in Judaism.) Conflicting versions of Christian values, as opposed to any kind of consensus on them, have been projected into the public square and now compete to shape the values of Christians. This has weakened any sense of America having a shared Christian ethos. Christians don't even have a shared Christian ethos.

Meanwhile, new waves of immigration continue to bring greater and greater religious diversity to the nation. Adherents of all the major world religions have come here in large number. To the extent that some of these immigrants are adherents of non-Christian religions, their increasing presence stokes anxiety among those wishing for that earlier, more Christian America.

Though the United States remains a predominantly Christian culture in terms of the religious affiliation of its adherents (around 70 percent), American cultural Christianity is definitely giving way to something for which we do not yet have a name. Our people, and therefore our expressions of public culture, are more pluralistic, more diverse, more secular, more post-institutional-religion, and more morally divided. This state of affairs has destabilized our political culture, leading to heightened division and anxiety. The cultural strength of Christianity no longer deeply affects legislation—at least not everywhere and not univocally. Cultural progressives now have the power at some times and in some places to advance legislation that traditional-minded Christians see as a fundamental violation of their values. Good examples include abortion, assisted suicide, and gay marriage. This collapse of the old cultural Christianity at the national level has come as quite a shock, most especially in regions where Christian cultural establishment was and remains strongest. The values conflicts undercut the perceived moral legitimacy of the federal government and create despair about the direction of America.

The broadly Christian political culture that once existed in America helped Christians feel comfortable for two centuries in not using their cultural power directly to undercut legal disestablishment. But the erosion of that political culture has also motivated some Christians to attempt to rally the vestiges of their cultural power, especially where it is strongest, to achieve symbolic and policy gains in advancing what they would say are simply America's core Judeo-Christian values and what to their opponents looks like legal establishment of the Christian religion (and its morality). Some of these efforts have succeeded, others have not, but the effects have been felt nonetheless.

Can America's Christians find a better way forward in these anxious times? I do not dare to hope for any kind of recovery of a religious or moral consensus or near consensus. Nor do I hope for some kind of traditional Christian resurgence or conservative political movement to "take back America." Our divisions are too deep, our differences too entrenched, and the raw exercise of political power by Christians to coerce adherence to values many people have abandoned would be both bad governance and bad Christian witness.

For America's Christians, our only real way forward is in actually living out our faith (including its core moral values) with fidelity and in finding winsome, appealing ways to share that faith with our neighbors, beginning with our own children. Christian faith had such a powerful hold on the American people for so long because earlier generations of Christians, pastors, and churches found a way to tell and live the Christian story that drew millions of people into Christian commitment. Meanwhile, although there are policy issues on which we will have to take a stand, we need to accept that the public culture of our more diverse and secular country is unlikely ever to return to cultural Christianity as we once knew it and as so many yearn for it to be again.

Chapter 3

DEMOCRACY

A Christian Way to Govern?

MANY AMERICANS ARE DEEPLY FRUSTRATED WITH THE functioning of our government, especially at the national level. Nothing ever seems to get done. The parties are at each other's throats all the time. They can't agree on even the simplest matters. And when they can agree, it usually seems to involve borrowing more money or finding other "solutions" that kick the can down the road until the next time a decision has to be made.

The structure of our government itself seems to favor inactivity. Two houses of Congress have to agree on legislation before it can go to the president. The Senate is especially difficult to get through because most bills now require at least sixty votes, and in many cases a single recalcitrant senator can prevent consideration of a matter on the Senate floor. If somehow a bill can get to the president, he or she can veto it, and it is even more difficult to override a veto. And anything that does get through all those hurdles can be (and often is) challenged in court, which can temporarily or permanently block signed bills from being executed in real life.

All Americans are (or used to be) taught about our brilliant founders and the marvels of our democratic system. But cynicism about the actual functioning of our government in the present is high and has fueled the rise of protest candidates in many elections. Something seems to be very wrong. Our delicately balanced constitutional system with its checks and balances may be beyond the capacity of the current generation of Americans, or at least American politicians, to manage. The hardening of our two-party system into a two-hatreds system, the rise of lobbyists and interest groups, the spectacle of 24/7 media coverage, the role of big money in politics, the dominance of personal ambition over concern for the common good—all this may be contributing to the gradual erosion of our once well-functioning democracy.

As Christians, it helps to remember that American-style democracy was a relatively late arrival on the human stage and that it cannot claim any unequivocal biblical mandate. Old Testament Israel was a theocracy, a tribal league, a theocratic monarchy, and an occupied province of ancient world empires, never a democracy. Christians in the New Testament era never had governing power, of course, and only a small number were citizens under imperial Rome. The internal governance of the churches does not appear to have been especially democratic, though the picture is not monochromatic. The structure depicted in later New Testament writings such as 1 Timothy and Titus seems more hierarchical than, for example, what existed in the church at Corinth.

The most sustained effort to offer a theology of the state in the New Testament is found in the apostle Paul's exhortation in Romans 13:1–7. This passage is controversial, in part because of its apparent blithe confidence that the Roman state should be viewed as established by God, fulfilling divine purposes in the world, and worthy of Christian submission. It cast a long shadow for many centuries. It taught Christians to think of the state as established by God, its rulers placed on their thrones by God, its task to keep order and prevent wickedness through violence and the threat thereof, and its fearsome power to be meekly obeyed by Christians—except, perhaps, when it overreaches and attempts to mandate idolatry or renunciation of Christ. There is no theology of citizenship in Romans 13, no idea that the state derives its just powers from the consent of those it governs, no theory of justified resistance, no separation of powers or checks and balances, as in modern democratic theory.

The appeal of more-authoritarian models of government has consistently reappeared in Christian thought and practice. These have been undoubtedly fueled by a primal image of God as Divine King, reinforced by centuries of "Christian" emperors and kings claiming to be God's representatives on earth, and modeled by hierarchical church structures involving popes, cardinals, bishops, and pastors lording it over their people.

The idea of a genuinely democratic style of church governance comes late in Christian history, resides predominantly in the free-church tradition on the left wing of the Reformation, and has always been a minority voice within broader Christendom.

On reviewing the ravages of the twentieth century, it is troubling to notice that the right-wing fascists and dictatorships that developed in midcentury Europe were often attractive to Christians and church authorities. Mussolini's Italy, Franco's Spain, Hitler's Germany (not to mention Vichy France and wartime Slovakia), found considerable support among authoritarian-leaning Christians. Democracy gave way to dictatorship in these countries in part because democracy was seen as weak and inefficient in addressing grave national problems and in part because these societies were not deeply and ineradicably committed to democracy. Centuries of authoritarian religion underwriting authoritarian government regimes had much to do with that.

Perhaps because I am a Baptist, and thus heir to a democratic free-church tradition, and perhaps because I have done considerable writing about the twentieth century's tyrannical regimes, I have been inoculated against the appeal of authoritarianism. Certainly any human structure needs strong and effective leadership, whether it is a business, a family, a church, or a nation. But leaders are sinful humans, too, and the more power they have, the more they need people with countervailing power to keep them from abusing those they are supposed to be leading. Leaders can easily become tyrants. That is a core insight undergirding our system of government, and it is why everybody in government is checked by everybody else—and by a free press and a free people.

George Washington was a compelling leader, so compelling that he needed a system around him to keep him from becoming the next King George. And he himself needed a commitment to letting go of power, not holding onto it—a commitment he acted on. He has been followed by 240 years of leaders who have retained the same commitment and by a political culture that has resisted the appeal of authoritarians, tyrants, and demagogues. May it ever be so.

Christians have a role in participating in the American democratic process to ensure that it is as healthy as it can be. Only 60 percent of Americans tend to vote even in the most contested presidential elections. This is a scandal. In off-year elections, the numbers are much smaller. And democratic participation drops to miniscule proportions when it comes to such basic citizenship responsibilities as contacting representatives, attending protests or rallies, posting opinions online or in the newspaper, or supporting and participating in the myriad civil-society organizations that constantly monitor the health of our democracy.

There are certain basic reforms of the current functioning of our democracy that Christians can advocate. Congressional districts should be drawn up by nonpartisan commissions, not self-interested politicians and parties. Senate rules should be altered so that more legislation can pass with a simple majority. Our political parties need the more active participation of centrist and moderate voters so that they are not constantly pulled to the right or left. The creaky old Electoral College system needs reconsideration so that every voter matters in a presidential election, not just those in six or eight "swing states." Voting needs to be made easier, not harder, for all American citizens to ensure the greatest participation. The financing of our political campaigns needs to be as transparent as possible, and the power of big corporate money needs to be reined in. The quasi-official role of the Republican and Democratic parties needs to be fought. A strong, free, independent press must be protected. And so on.

Democracy is not *the* Christian way to govern. But it reflects core Christian insights: the value of the individual, protection of minorities and the vulnerable, broad political participation reflecting the dignity and worth of all, and careful limits to any one person's power. American democracy has never been perfect. It has also never been static. It is a living thing, dynamic, always evolving, sometimes and in some ways for the better, sometimes and in some ways for the worse. It is sustained by a culture, a culture with a deep democratic ethos and the institutions that support it. This ethos must be protected, along with the democracy it exists to nurture. Christians have a crucial role to play.

Chapter 4

PARTIES

What Do We Make of Today's Democrats and Republicans?

THERE IS NO LAW THAT SAYS AMERICA SHALL HAVE TWO political parties and their names shall be Republican and Democrat. In fact, the founders were suspicious of political parties, worrying that they would contribute to factionalism and division. It looks like they were, as the Brits say, spot-on about that. But today it is not just that these two political parties have become quasi-official, wired into our governing system in ways that could never have been envisioned by our founders. They have also become great temptations for Christians who would like to be able to align their political and religious loyalties without any jagged edges, even though this is impossible—especially with the two parties we have now.

Let's think about the absurdity of the American two-party system for just a moment. What we really have are two nongovernmental, or quasi-governmental, entities that exert enormous public power but that are beyond the control of the people of the United States. We do not elect their leaders, nor can we recall them. We do not set their budgets, nor can we alter them. We do not establish their policy platforms, nor can we revise them. We do not determine which candidates they will fund and support. We do not establish their primary systems at presidential election time. We, like sheep, must accept whatever they, like dueling monarchs, dole out to us. Who said it had to be done this way? Why should we accept it? Is it actually working for us?

These parties, and their fiercest adherents, now hate each other deeply. But they do have some profound shared interests. Their fundamental shared interest is in the status quo that ensures that the United States will have two extremely powerful quasi-official parties that will continue in that role year after year, decade after decade. Neither party wants to give up their ruling duopoly. Neither party wants to see a transformation of our system to a multiparty one in which they will have to compete with others for offices up and down the ballot. Neither wants to see viable third parties or even viable self-funded independent candidates. As they do their dance of mutual contempt, they do it together, leaving all others out, all other possibilities unthinkable.

The stranglehold of this two-parties-only situation long preceded the modern culture wars. And for a time, the left/right polarization of our politics was not perfectly reflected in the agendas of the parties. In my lifetime (which I admit is getting to be a long lifetime), there have been liberal Republicans and conservative Democrats. But over time, the two parties have grown to represent pretty fixed right-wing and left-wing options. The polarization is most visible on social/moral and economic policy issues, where Republicans are moralistic on social policy and laissez-faire on economic policy, and Democrats are moralistic on economic policy and laissez-faire on social policy. The foreign policy situation is a bit more fluid, though in general Republicans are more prone to support military action and Democrats are more diplomacy oriented.

There is no obvious match between the agenda of either party and the agenda of the Bible or of Jesus himself. In part that's because each party is funded by people whose interests determine the agenda of the parties and whose power is so great that the parties must align with them. In both parties, Big Money dominates, though it comes from different subcultures of America's rich. And both parties have blind spots that leave certain policy options—such as completely abolishing the death penalty or engaging in a serious effort to address systemic poverty—beyond the realm of the possible.

This does not stop deep-dyed partisans from identifying their party's victory with the victory of their liberal or conservative god, election after election. Many Christians do this, more often these days on the right than on the left, but you can see it on both sides. Think about the cozy marriage of social conservative Christians with the GOP (God's Own Party, right?) and of black-church leaders with the Democrats. We have warnings about this kind of confusion and conflation in the Bible, and they are stern ones: "You shall have no other gods before me" and "Do not take the name of the Lord your God in vain"—in other words, what happens every day when religion and politics converge.

So what is an anxious Christian to do? At one level, as citizens we need to do our best to break the power of the quasi-governmental two-party system. We certainly need to remind ourselves and others that this system we have inherited is neither inevitable nor ideal. And for as long as the menu available to us in our national political cafeteria consists of exactly two items, we need to resist party idolatry. We need to keep our critical distance and evaluate each party and each candidate from a consistently Christian perspective, to the best of our ability. We must never turn politicians into messianic figures or give undue loyalty to any political party. And when people around us get this wrong—especially if they are pastors or religious leaders—we need to call them on it. Our rigid two-party system is part of what is wrong with our country, part of what makes me an anxious Christian. These are at least a few things we can do to challenge its power and work toward a better day.

Recent elections have seen the rise of outsider candidates, usually from the far sides of the ideological spectrum, whose success comes at the expense of candidates endorsed by party elites. It may be that newly emerging factors—including 24/7 cable TV coverage, obsessive polling, high-profile preprimary debates, social media, celebrity politics, voter anger, and ideological polarization—are wrestling control of the two parties away from those who are accustomed to leading them. Not only is this process delivering the most politically polarized candidates we've seen in some time, but it may mean the end of the parties as we know them. The concerns articulated above about the two-party system are real; what replaces it, however, may bring its own very real concerns as well.

Chapter 5

FRACTURES

Portrait of a Divided Country

OUR NATION IS BADLY DIVIDED. THERE ARE DIFFERENT types of divisions, but the one I want to discuss here is usually signaled by the term *culture wars*. People generally understand that term to mean that we have cultural liberals and cultural conservatives and that they really do not like or even understand each other. These divisions create extraordinary anxiety, especially when they come home—such as when a church or denomination divides over the LGBT issue or when Thanksgiving dinner is ruined by a political argument. Certainly our culture-war divisions create acute anxieties, and not only among Christians. Let's think about what's going on and how we got here.

Polarization is a descriptive word for what we are facing. It is as if two all-powerful magnets, one to our left and the other to our right, seem to grab most Americans and pull us in one direction or the other. Hardly anyone seems exempt.

One way to break this down might be to identify the polarization as having political, cultural, and religious dimensions. Those on the left are on the left *politically*, identifying as progressive or liberal on all different kinds of policy issues and voting Democratic (or to the Bernie-Sanders-left-of-Democratic). They are on the left *culturally*, by which I mean supporting cultural change rather than conserving the status quo, with a focus on the inclusion of more and more previously marginalized groups and on breaking the power of the originally most powerful group in the United States: white Christian men of European descent. And they are on the left *religiously*, which sometimes means holding traditional doctrinal or ethical positions loosely or abandoning them altogether. The same thing, in reverse, would hold true for those on the right.

I offer a Baptist example. Those on the (white) Baptist left, at least in the South, identify as progressive or liberal and overwhelmingly vote Democratic (and almost always choose losing candidates). They favor full equality for women in the churches and generally embrace the social change and social justice agenda of the left. They sometimes hold loosely to some traditional doctrinal or ethical positions. They almost always identify with Baptist leaders such as Social Gospel leader Walter Rauschenbusch, civil rights icon Martin Luther King Jr., and former president Jimmy Carter.

The Baptist right, on the other hand, identifies as politically conservative and overwhelmingly votes

Republican. They generally do not support women's ordination and reject most or all of the social change and social justice agenda of the left. (Race makes for an interesting exception.) They hold tightly to pretty much all traditional doctrinal and ethical positions. They identify with Baptist leaders such as theologian Carl F. H. Henry, former Nixon aide and born-again activist Chuck Colson, and former Arkansas governor Mike Huckabee.

It is precisely the comprehensiveness of the polarization that is so striking. There is no intrinsic reason why just about every aspect of the life of a religious person or group should fly to the left or the right as if by magnetic attraction. This appears mostly to be a U.S. phenomenon, and a distinctively contemporary one.

So what happened that got us to this point?

The first major analysis of the situation we are still facing in America was offered by sociologist James Davison Hunter in his groundbreaking book *Culture Wars: The Struggle to Define America* (New York: Basic Books, 1991). Hunter described the situation as a clash of worldviews between groups he called "orthodox" and "progressive" (equivalent to "right" and "left"). These groups, especially as embodied by their activists, differ over "our most fundamental and cherished assumptions about how to order our lives" individually and in society (p. 42). These are "competing moral visions" so distinct as to create "polarizing impulses or tendencies" throughout American culture, even though "most Americans occupy a vast middle ground" (p. 43). One wonders whether he would still make that claim today.

According to Hunter, competing understandings of the source and nature of moral truth lie at the heart of the culture wars. These differences lead to different moral beliefs about a wide range of particular issues. They also tend to produce different postures toward culture as well as different political dispositions. Thus, on the one side are cultural conservatives and moral traditionalists, while on the other side are cultural and moral progressives or liberals.

At the time Hunter wrote his book, the alignment of the platforms and agendas of our two major political parties with these two sides of the culture wars had not progressed nearly as far as it has today. Though there are certainly still many exceptions, such as pro-life Democrats and pro–gay rights Republicans, today the Democrats generally align with the culture wars' left and the Republicans with the culture wars' right. This is crystal clear during national presidential campaigns. It is somewhat less true state by state.

A more politically focused analysis with a somewhat longer time frame has been offered by Rick Perlstein in his trilogy on the rise of modern political conservatism. *Before the Storm* (New York: Nation Books, 2001) focuses on 1964 Republican presidential nominee Barry Goldwater and the circumstances preceding and surrounding his run. *Nixonland* (New York: Scribner, 2008) describes the career of the inimitable Richard Nixon but along the way offers a stunning description of America in the turbulent 1960s. Similarly, *The Invisible Bridge* (New York: Simon & Schuster, 2014) tells the story of the rise of Ronald Reagan to the presidency against the backdrop of the events of the 1970s.

Perlstein shows that the left/right polarization that we know so well is inextricable from the birth of the modern conservative movement in the 1950s. That movement began with two major pillars: staunch anticommunism in the context of the Cold War, often accompanied by support for a confrontational policy toward the nuclear-armed USSR; and small-government economic proposals in reaction to the policies of Franklin Roosevelt's New Deal.

The developments of the 1960s added a third major pillar: cultural conservatism. This cultural conservatism erupted in reaction to the sexual revolution, the gay rights movement, the women's movement, the drug culture, the widespread opposition to the Vietnam War, and racial integration and the civil rights movement. After 1973, the national decriminalization of abortion became a major new element on this list, and still more items were added as other culture-war battlegrounds emerged.

Barry Goldwater, Richard Nixon, and, most effectively, Ronald Reagan created a new Republican coalition and a new version of conservatism that combined all three of these pillars: staunch anticommunism (together with a hawkish foreign policy and American exceptionalism, unilateralism, and national pride), small-government/antitax/probusiness economics, and moral traditionalism on issues such as sex, drugs, family, and abortion. On race, the somewhat more veiled white conservative line was advanced through a variety of proxies such as opposition to affirmative action and to enforced school busing for racial integration.

Democrats, on the other hand, often (though not always) offered a softer foreign policy line while always offering a diametrically opposed set of economic policies, support for racial integration and "minority uplift" efforts (after the decline of the Southern Democrats), and a fairly consistent moral progressivism on sex, family, and abortion, if not drugs.

The culture wars have often been understood to include only the last element of this triad, but the pulling together of foreign and military policy, economic policy, and cultural issues defines the comprehensive political, moral, cultural, and even religious polarization that creates such angst today. Look at the Democratic and Republican party platforms of any election year, and they will generally fall in with these broad lines of demarcation, to which other issues could be added today, such as immigration, the Israel/Palestine conflict, and education reform.

The most recent major book I have seen on the subject, *A War for the Soul of America* (Chicago: University of Chicago Press, 2015), is by historian Andrew Hartman. Unlike Perlstein, Hartman locates the origins of the culture wars in the emergence of the New Left of the 1960s, with its challenges to traditional values already outlined.

Hartman then focuses his attention on a kind of two-stage conservative pushback. First came the neoconservatives, mainly Jews and Catholics such as Norman Podhoretz and Daniel Patrick Moynihan. In the early 1970s, they attacked the agenda of the New Left, especially on race, gender, and education. Later in the

1970s, the Protestant fundamentalists and evangelicals joined the neoconservatives in an uneasy coalition, bringing their characteristic concerns with such issues as abortion. This alignment has been consistently opposed by heirs to the New Left—and off we go into the conflict that has defined our era. Though Hartman suggests that the culture wars pretty much had wound down by the late 1990s, I think he is wrong, at least in the world I inhabit.

Our politics have hardened into semipermanent culture-war categories. Large parts of our media have joined the polarization. Social media only makes it worse. And many religious communities have simply splintered, formally or informally, along left/right lines. Through much of my career, I have hoped to contribute to a culture, or at least a church, that can get beyond such polarization. No Christian ought to see our capitulation to a relatively recent, very American, totally contingent polarization as anything other than a defeat for Christian integrity and unity, not to mention for cultural well-being.

Scanning the entire Christian landscape, I find in the Roman Catholic Church one of my only sources of hope. Catholicism has a long historical memory, so it knows better than to identify current circumstances with eternal truths. It is international, so it has resources for getting beyond parochially American categories and patterns. It has resources in theology and ethics that challenge simple left/right binaries. And it appears impervious to a full-blown institutional left/right split as might happen with a Protestant congregation or denomination. One of the very best things any anxious American Christian can do to respond to our social left/right fracture is to read some Catholic social teaching, with its conservatism on abortion and family and its progressivism on justice and peace issues. Pope Francis pretty much embodies that binary-smashing combination, which is why Americans were both dazzled and baffled when he visited in 2015.

Beyond that, all of us can do more to try to "walk a mile in the other's moccasins." We can get out of our informational and friendship ghettos. We can force ourselves to watch both Fox and MSNBC and to read both the *New York Times* and the *Wall Street Journal*. We can choose not to hold friendships hostage to political or cultural agreement. We can listen more, speak more softly, and always try to understand how others arrived at their views. A good test is whether we can restate what the other person has said in a way that shows we really understand it. We can refuse to demonize those with whom we disagree. And we can remember that this whole sprawling, squabbling assemblage of human beings is part of our country, and there is no chance that it will anytime soon be reduced to include only those who agree with us.

Chapter 6

JUDGES

They Didn't Sign Up for This

PITY THE POOR JUDGES. WE ASK SO MUCH OF THEM NOW. Because of the social fractures discussed in the last chapter, many of the issues that judges face are culture-war imbroglios: abortion, gay marriage, religious liberty. In so many cases, the forces of the mainly secular progressive left square off against the forces of the mainly Christian conservative right. It never stops.

The Supreme Court now serves as the final court of appeal for the culture wars. Our presidents ping-pong from left to right and right to left. Our legislatures are divided at the state and national level. Every substantial issue that tastes like the culture wars finds its ways to those nine robed justices who since *Marbury v. Madison* (1803) have offered the final word on the constitutionality of executive and legislative actions. It is a fearsome amount of power that falls on the shoulders of what was once called "the least dangerous branch" of government.

The judiciary would probably not be called that today, especially the Supreme Court, whose legitimacy has taken some significant blows from both the left and the right over the last fifty years or more. Think about it. Richard Nixon ran against the Warren Court in 1968 for being soft on crime, which often was code for being too friendly to minorities. It was the Warren Court, after all, that ushered in the explosion of social changes around race with its 1954 *Brown v. Board of Education* ruling, which mandated the integration of public schools. That same court gave us the Miranda rulings, which many of us memorized while watching *Dragnet* in the late 1960s: "You have the right to remain silent. Anything you say can and will be used against you." Amid the campus protests, street riots, and white backlash against racial integration, Richard Nixon played the Supreme Court card and won with it.

But the Court did not change overnight. Five years after Nixon was elected came the 7-2 *Roe v. Wade* decision, which overrode all contrary abortion laws and established what critics ever since have called "abortion on demand." It took a few years, but Christian Right activists seized on *Roe* to build a case against the "imperial judiciary" and for the election of Republican presidents who would move the Supreme Court to the religious and political right—and who would overturn *Roe*. Ronald Reagan and all subsequent successful Republican nominees ran on such promises, and they gradually populated the Court with a new conservative wing, consisting of the late Justice Antonin Scalia, along with Clarence Thomas, Samuel Alito, and to a lesser extent Chief Justice John Roberts. All were conservative Catholics, and in the case of the first three, it has not been hard to see the imprint of that conservative Catholicism on their case rulings.

But the Court itself is divided. Its liberal wing consists of three Jewish justices (Stephen Breyer, Elena Kagan, and Ruth Bader Ginsburg) and one left-leaning Catholic (Sonia Sotomayor), with moderate Catholic Anthony Kennedy as the pivotal swing vote. Protestants have to notice that for the first time in history there is not a single one of "us" on the Court. I am among those who have felt some anxiety about what this absence says about where U.S. Protestantism is and where our country is going.

The legitimacy of the Supreme Court and other lower courts depends on the perception that they are interpreting the Constitution and the cases and controversies before them using recognized and widely agreed-upon jurisprudential principles. Citizens need to be able to believe that the Constitution reigns supreme in the Supreme Court; that legal rather than partisan, political, ideological, moralistic, or religious reasoning is being employed; that precedents are being taken seriously; that the Court is relating to the other branches (and to the states) with appropriate respect. The more the Court is required to resolve highly politicized culture-war cases, the more the perception of the Court's legitimacy is threatened.

One reason for concern can be found in the Court's own recent dissents. For example, the dissents of Justice

Scalia in the *Obergefell v. Hodges* gay marriage decision, as well as in the *National Federation of Independent Business v. Sebelius* case related to the Affordable Care Act, were so scathing they could feed the perception that he viewed the results as not just wrong but illegitimate. That is dangerous ground in a society as divided as ours. Certainly the gay marriage decision has evoked howls of outrage and even acts of defiance among some charged with enforcing it. Of course, the same thing happened sixty years earlier with the *Brown* school integration decision, with resistance sufficiently powerful to delay any real implementation of school integration for a decade or more. With partisanship and culture-war divisions as deep as they are, with many acts of (whichever) Congress and (whichever) president viewed as illegitimate by their adversaries, the viability of our democracy sometimes seems to hang on the slenderest of reeds—those nine justices at the Supreme Court. This offers good reasons for sleepless nights for all of us.

The sudden death of Justice Scalia in February 2016 only heightened the intensity of these concerns. News of his death had hardly been out for an hour before partisan divisions had already surfaced. The Republican Senate told President Obama not to bother to send up a nominee; the president told the press that of course he would do so. The next day's *New York Times* gave Justice Scalia's death one of its exceedingly rare banner headlines. This is simply way too much pressure to put on one part of one branch of our government—on nine human beings. We are at serious risk here.

So what is an anxious Christian to do? All of this stuff seems way over the heads of the average Christian.

But culture matters, and everything we say and do as Christians contributes to culture. What to do? One thing we can do is to avoid the language of *legitimacy* when expressing unhappiness with Supreme Court decisions that we don't like. We can strongly disagree if we must, but we must not add fuel to the fire of those who say a decision is simply illegitimate and unlawful and needs to be defied. Perhaps a time for such a response will come, but we had all better hesitate before jumping off that ledge.

Another step we can take is to read actual Supreme Court decisions and dissents rather than simply reading the headlines. At least most of the time, real legal reasoning is going on rather than dark partisan maneuvering. We can also pay attention to Supreme Court appointments. We can use whatever platform we have to advocate for the sharpest and fairest legal minds rather than anything less than that. All appointees will have some kind of ideological leanings; however, let's advocate for those who are not known for their ideology but instead for the quality of their legal scholarship. Finally, let's not pin our hopes for America's salvation—however we understand it—on the latest Supreme Court appointment or decision. That's too much to ask. It's bad theology. And it's bad to put that much pressure on those nine people who have too much expected of them already.

7

CHARACTER

Freedom under Discipline

A GOVERNMENT IS ONLY AS GOOD AS ITS PEOPLE, AND A people get the government they more or less deserve. These kinds of thoughts have run through my mind a lot recently as I have seen the repeated expressions of discontent among Americans about our government and its leaders. I keep wondering whether the problem isn't *them* but *us*.

Our system of government leans heavily in the direction of personal freedom. It still feels pretty much like what the English philosopher John Locke and others had in mind with their concept of government as a kind of primal social contract. (Locke's philosophy was, after all, highly influential at the time our nation was founded.) Individuals are free and would prefer to remain free. If they did not need some form of central authority to secure them from threats to their persons and property, there would be no government at all. But there are such threats, so people voluntarily, if reluctantly, cede just enough of their autonomy in order to enjoy a reasonable amount of security. Government exists to provide this security and perhaps a small range of other common goods. But government exists by the will of the governed, and its mandate is limited. In every other aspect of life except for that which free people have contracted for government regulation, they remain free to direct their own lives without interference from others.

What results from this kind of vision—or at least, what resulted in our country—is a political culture in which the default setting is to maximize freedom. Freedom of speech, freedom of the press, freedom of association, freedom of movement, freedom of religion, freedom of commerce and exchange, freedom to create and dissolve just about any form of human endeavor one can imagine—this is the American way of life. Many people who have suffered under tyrannies of various types have come to our shores attracted by this expansive vision of freedom.

But today many Christians are anxious about a transition from freedom to chaos, from liberty to license, in the actual daily character of our country. Freedom is a great thing, except for when people misuse it. Freedom of speech is great except for when people use it to curse and slander others. Freedom of the press is great except for when the press libels people. Freedom of association is great except for when people form hate groups. Freedom of religion is great except for when their religion does harm to others or to their own children. Freedom to form and dissolve romantic relationships is great except for when people bring harm to themselves and others who count on them. Commercial freedom is great except for when business harms people with unsafe products. And so on.

It is clear that America's founders understood that the freedom-maximizing government they were creating required a citizenry of sound character to go along with it. Government could stay small and limited if, and only if, people could regulate their own actions in virtuous ways. You don't need a whole lot of police in a town in which 99.9 percent of the citizenry on a given day are choosing not to break the laws that their representatives have established. Virtuous business owners don't cheat their customers or mistreat their employees, so government does not need to get involved in that arena very much. Spouses of sound mind and character do not physically harm their children or each other, so, again, government can remain minimally involved in the affairs of most families. And so on.

For centuries, religion has been one primary force undergirding the formation of character. In the United States at the time of our founding, of course, the primary religion was Christianity, in various forms. The founders counted on the force of Christianity to shape and constrain the exercise of freedom by most Americans. Even those who had left the theology of Christianity behind were still affected by the broadly Christian ethos that Christians and their churches had formed here. That formative power manifested itself in many ways, among them Christian preaching, home-by-home

parental Bible teaching, the formation of human conscience, and the belief that everyone must someday
give account of their lives to God. Of course, the same
thing happened and still happens in many other cultures in which a deep and widespread religiosity per-
vades community, family, and personal values.

I think we have good reason at this time in our long
national sojourn to be anxious about the erosion of
the moral (and religious) ethos that once formed and
constrained our expressions of the maximized liberty
of our political system. The delicate balance that the
founders expected—a free people, but not utterly free,
because they are shaped and constrained by the force
of a powerfully religious and moral culture—is in the
process of being lost.

We can see the effects of that erosion in a variety
of places. I think it is especially clear in much of what
passes for entertainment. Liberty has become license;
entertainment has become degradation. Of course,
it's not just in the media. Don't miss the utterly ruthless business practices of many in corporate America,
or the anything-goes ethos of our political fighting to
see a similar loss of moral restraint. There used to be
certain things that decent people just did not do. This
baseline is eroding across the board.

Have you ever dealt with the criminal justice system? One of the first things you notice about it is how
little freedom there is. Even a visit to traffic court intro-
duces you to a world of stern directives, glaring large
men with big guns on their hips, and interesting intro-
ductions to the glories of the probation system. And
that's just traffic court. Try visiting a prison, and you

see environments in which tiny little bits of freedom are doled out as incentives or withdrawn as punishment. Such forays into the maw of the criminal justice system are a reminder at least of this: those who misuse their freedom lose it. Societies in which larger and larger numbers of people do not feel constrained by moral rules will find themselves requiring a heavier hand from government. And government forces can easily slip loose of their own legal and moral constraints if they are not carefully monitored and controlled. I believe we are seeing all the above in America right now.

So there is reason for Christians to be anxious about freedom giving way to license and, in response, small government giving way to big government. More police, more heavily armed police, more jails, more people on probation, more family court, more juvenile court, more lawsuits, more regulations to keep us from doing harm to each other—this is the new American way. That small grant of power from virtuous citizen to limited government to provide a measure of security seems like a long time ago in a galaxy far, far away.

Christians need a renewal of moral seriousness in our own lives. We need to retrieve religious resources easily available to us for the cultivation of character, such as the virtues taught by Jesus and found in the rest of the New Testament. We need to be able to draw a distinction between liberty and license. We need to remember the bracing moral teachings of the New Testament, which never envision anything like pure, unfettered freedom but instead only a choice of masters: God or self, Jesus or the evil one. We need creative ways to speak the language of character so that our children and grandchildren will be able to understand what we mean and want it for themselves. We need to be brave enough to push back against the most egregious cultural expressions of raw degradation masquerading as entertainment. And we need to look for leaders in every venue—family, church, business, community, national government—who exemplify qualities of character such as honesty, discipline, self-control, unselfishness, patience, forgiveness, humility, mercy, and covenant faithfulness.

8

PATRIOTISM

(How) Should Christians Love America?

I KNOW EXACTLY WHEN IT DAWNED ON ME HOW MUCH I love America. It was in 2005, when I was offered and nearly accepted a post associated with Cambridge University in England. Most academics would kill for such an offer, because most of us romanticize those grand British universities. (And those accents! Everyone just sounds so smart over there.)

But I turned the offer down. There were many reasons, but one of them was that I could not bring myself to leave the good old USA. This tug to stay home was so powerful, so surprising, that it made me think a bit more deeply about its component parts. When I did that, my patriotism seemed to have three main dimensions: place, identity, and service.

America is my place, the spot in the world that I call home, the place where I belong and to which I always yearn to return when I am away. Ironically, my family's love for travel and extensive experience overseas has heightened both my appreciation for the wider world and my sense of home when I hit American soil.

Being American is part of my identity, who I am as a human being. There are certainly many other parts of my identity—I am a husband and father, a son and uncle and brother and grandfather, an Atlanta sports fan and baseball aficionado, a teacher and writer, a classic movie lover, and an enjoyer of bookstores. And above all, I am, or seek to be, a follower of Jesus Christ. The American part of my identity is so strong that it could no more be laid aside, even temporarily, than could other core aspects of my identity.

I feel a strong desire to serve America. I want to understand the history and culture of this nation as well as I can, and I want to do my part to help it be the best nation that it can be. For me, the desire to serve my country never took the form of military service, though it did for my father and my father-in-law. But I serve my country through what I am doing in this book and in most of my work—namely, trying to contribute to healing, understanding, and justice in our civic culture and trying to help America's still-majority Christian population be the best version of ourselves in this anxious time.

Substantial voices in Christian thought have argued strongly against any affirmation of patriotism. They see it as a dangerous temptation to idolatry. They worry about the many "God = America = Jesus" mash-ups that we have witnessed in the history of this culturally

Christian land. Or they look overseas to our European forebears and remember the grotesque wars of religion that took so many lives in the name of one or another version of Christianity. They remember that all those European Christian nations went into World War I, and even to some extent World War II, with "God" on their side.

A much-needed critique of the centrality of the nation-state has surfaced broadly in Christian scholarship in recent decades. After all, the nation-state as we know it is a late arrival on the scene. Such states spend an awful lot of blood and money defining and contesting their borders, as well as defining and contesting who counts as a member of the nation-state community. Who's to say that our loyalties should be national at all? Why not local, or regional, if one wants to claim loyalty to a place at all? And aren't Christians supposed to be the ultimate internationalists, since we are members of an international church ("We believe in the one, holy, catholic, and apostolic church"), we believe all people are made in the image of God, we serve one God who is sovereign over all the universe, and nationality has no place in Christian doctrine whatsoever? As the kids would say—Boom!

At one level, to hold on to a concept of patriotic loyalty after this critique is a matter of realism. We live in a world in which nation-states still matter. They exist at just one level of a multifaceted array of human social organizations, but this level remains an important one. Every human being remains a citizen of a particular nation-state and finds legal protection within that country, as is evidenced most painfully when people end up as stateless refugees and find they have no one to succor them when they are in trouble. Perhaps one day humanity will evolve to such a place that nation-states will become obsolete. It hasn't happened yet, however.

Accepting patriotic loyalty, even among Christians, also speaks a word of realism about the way human identity actually works. Each of us, in fact, combines multiple identities. As Christians, we can and should do our prayerful best to order our identities around our central identity as followers of Jesus Christ. This takes much training, over a lifetime. But the effort to cauterize our subidentities to our central one, such as our identity as citizens of one nation or another, is in most cases a fool's errand. If it has not been permitted open expression, national loyalty will probably surface in a veiled way.

But the most important reason to embrace patriotic loyalty is to bring it into subjection to the love of neighbor that Christ commanded. If we are serious about loving our neighbors, this must include those neighbors with whom we share local, state, regional, and national community. And one of the things that most intimately affects those neighbors is the vitality, character, and governance of the national community in which we all live.

This is why Christian patriotism needs to be a critical, service-oriented, love-centered loyalty. It is definitely not a "my country right or wrong" patriotism. It isn't an "Our military is so strong it can kick everyone else's butt" patriotism. It isn't a "We must preserve domination of America by white people" patriotism. And it isn't a "Let's use our power to dominate our weaker neighbors economically" patriotism. It's more like a "Let's redeem the promise of America for all Americans" patriotism, such as was articulated so beautifully by one of America's greatest patriots, Dr. Martin Luther King Jr.

It is reasonable to wonder where the greater danger lies—in the wrong forms of patriotism or in resignation from patriotism into either high-minded internationalism or a disengaged focus on ourselves. Think about how even the most highly contested and publicized presidential elections draw barely half of voting-eligible Americans to the polls. The others are free riders as their neighbors carry out the most basic civic responsibilities. Yes, our country, including our political process, is deeply, maddeningly, outrageously flawed. Therefore, precisely as followers of Christ, let's roll up our sleeves in exercising our citizenship responsibilities as faithfully as we can.

Chapter 9

RACE

One White Christian Tries to Figure It Out

OUR NATION HAS SUBSTANTIAL, CHRONIC, AND PAINFUL racial problems. About this there can be little doubt. What do we see, what should we see, when we look at race in America?

We should see that the domination of U.S. politics, culture, and economic life by people (especially men) of European background (i.e., "white" people) has been one of the most fundamental structural realities of American life.

We were a colonial outpost of the seventeenth century. The European colonizers essentially destroyed the Native American populations it discovered here. They simultaneously developed the institution of chattel slavery of African people and maintained this system for over 250 years until it was legally abolished after the Civil War.

White racism was a precursor to what happened in American history, and its deepening was one result of events here. By that I mean that it required a certain kind of Eurocentric, white-people-centric worldview—a certain kind of mental construction of human civilization involving a hierarchy of human beings along racial lines—for the Europeans to act as they did in the lands that they conquered and settled. This racist worldview did not originate here, nor were its results visible only here. It manifested itself everywhere the Europeans went, all over the world. It is a definitive part of the worldwide colonial experience.

Slavery was a peculiarly egregious manifestation of white European, and eventually Euro-American, racism. We know that indentured servitude was not confined to black people in the earliest colonial period. But eventually slavery became a white-on-black victimization, and its justification took on a deeply racialized hue. It obviously took quite a bit of racism to begin enslaving people on a racial basis, and quite a bit more to maintain the practice of slavery in the face of the manifest humanity, dignity, and suffering of slaves whom one encountered at close hand most every day. This deep racism, which consisted of denying the evidence visible right before one's eyes, deeply damaged the moral sensibility of America's white people, most especially those who owned slaves and/or defended slavery. It was also a direct affront to the supposed Christian commitments of the vast majority of slaveholders. Living with that contradiction required a systematic elimination of the social justice elements of Christian faith and a systematic searing of the consciences of white Christian people. It is not too much to say that we have been blinded by racism, beginning with being blind to its existence and its effects both on us and on our victims.

This is how white racism became a deeply woven part of American culture, so deep that it has proven impossible to eradicate it entirely, even 150 years since the end of the Civil War. Every advance for black people has been met by determined white opposition and has inflamed that opposition. Every year brings fresh evidence of the systemic permeation of racism into pretty much every corner of American life: policing, business, housing, health, environment, politics, employment, wealth building, education. One very rare exception, it seems to me, comes in those sectors of society that are so purely results-oriented that racism would stand in the way of an even more core value. Take, for example, sports, where (only for the last five decades or less) almost always the best players are put on the field, regardless of skin tone. The military is another great example. White people often seem to want to believe that every sector of society is just like the sports world and the military. But that is simply not the case.

This founding racism based on explicit beliefs about the superiority of white people of European descent has worked itself out in relation to all other ethnicities here. The specifics of how and why this racism has expressed itself vary, of course. And by now, with the cultural discrediting of most expressions of blatant, open racism, much racism has gone underground—perhaps invisible even to those who are still affected by it.

Most issues we fight about today that have a racial component are one or two steps removed from the earlier, morally cleaner, and simpler battles. For example, the fight over what types of affirmative action to deploy in university admission processes is a subtler and more complex matter than whether slavery should be permitted or black people be given the vote. The proper shape of U.S. immigration policy is a complex matter that has racial dimensions to it but is not solely a racial issue. This makes it all the easier for even well-intentioned white people to express attitudes or to support policies on these kinds of issues that might be tinged with racism visible to others but not to them.

People who feel attacked as immoral tend to respond either with a disempowering sense of shame or with an angry defensiveness. I have seen plenty of both in my sojourns among America's white people. The ashamed group is still sometimes called "guilty white liberals," ever trying to expiate their racist sins and never quite succeeding. The latter group could be called "angry white reactionaries," not to put too fine a point on it. The thinking of both is often distorted, because we are not at our most rational when we are either ashamed or angry.

I have not attempted to speak directly to nonwhite Americans in this brief reflection. I think that most thoughtful black, Latino, Asian, and other people understand these realities, at least implicitly, a whole lot better than white people do. This is called the epistemological privilege of the oppressed—those without (unjust) power understand the workings of that power more clearly than those who have it. They see more clearly because their sense of moral well-being and self-worth does not require them to lie to themselves about what is really going on. I have found it amazing how much grace has been offered to me, and to other white Christian people, by nonwhite Christians I have had the privilege to know and serve alongside.

So my counsel here is predominantly for white Christians who are anxious and perhaps angry about accusations of white racism and who are baffled by all the issues tinged with race-talk, from police shootings to university admissions to immigration.

Listen closely to those voices outside your immediate family and friendship group, which in most cases in this country is still largely monochromatic. Don't turn off the TV when you encounter yet another race-related event that people are arguing about or crying out in distress about. Assume that you don't fully understand what it is like to live in nonwhite skin in this country, and try to learn as much as you can when you can. Listen closely to the stated policy agendas of nonwhite activists and policymakers to see what their priorities are.

Believe that the scholars are right when they say that privilege tends to blind the privileged, and so look hard for your own blind spots. Recall situations in which you were on the receiving end of mistreatment and remember how clear it was to you that it was wrong—but probably not to those who mistreated you. Study each issue that has a racial dimension with a willingness to take that racial dimension seriously, while paying attention to other dimensions of the issues as well. Ask whether you have fully considered those parts of the message of Jesus and the Christian faith that simply demand compassion, love, and justice for all—and that inspire you to live that way. Seize the opportunity to build or deepen interracial friendships and conversations, and don't get discouraged when something goes wrong or when you accidentally put your foot in your mouth.

In my experience, piercing the racial veil so that one arrives first at some mutual understanding, then at real interracial friendship, and finally at a place of free and easy "beloved community" across racial lines is a long journey, with many inevitable missteps. Keep at it. It's a crucial part of being a faithful Christian, and a constructive citizen, in America today.

Chapter 10

POLICE

Has It Always Been This Bad?

AS WE SAW EARLIER, SOCIAL-CONTRACT THEORY SAYS THAT the state exists because of a reluctant bow to necessity on the part of free people who discover there is one thing they cannot take care of alone—namely, securing themselves against wicked people who would harm them. So they give up a measure of freedom to a central authority with sufficient power to deter and punish those who would attack their neighbors.

Maybe you don't believe that story or are concerned about its implications. Perhaps as a Christian you prefer Paul's account in Romans 13. There God establishes authorities of all types, but especially state or governmental authority, to deter bad conduct and to punish it if necessary. Paul (in)famously says that "rulers are not a terror to good conduct, but to bad" (Rom. 13:3). So if you don't want to get in trouble with the authorities, don't do anything wrong, and all will be well for you.

A polite reading of this passage could conclude that Paul was offering a normative rather than descriptive account, which means that he was saying how things *should be* under God's sovereignty, not how they actually *are*. It has been argued that Paul was trying to tamp down any hint of Christian antigovernmental rebellion in a delicate situation in Rome, and so he framed his comments to that end. It is even possible that Paul wanted to sound as obedient and nonthreatening on the issue of government authority as he could, given the real possibility that his letter might be read by authorities in Rome. And it could be that by making such a straightforward claim about what a (just) government does with its (coercive) power, he was at least implicitly teaching any Roman authorities who might be paying attention what it was they should and should not be doing.

A less polite reading of this passage could conclude that Paul at this particular moment showed a blind spot about how state power actually works, at least against those who have little power in a society. In his famous book *Jesus and the Disinherited* (1949), Howard Thurman concludes that Paul writes as he does on state authority because of his privileged position as a Roman citizen. Thurman further argues that Jesus, a disenfranchised Galilean Jew, could not and did not view Roman power in the way Paul does here.

Of course, eventually Paul discovered how little protection his Roman citizenship provided him. Like his Lord, Paul also died under Roman state power. The state did in fact "bear the sword in vain." The state did prove to be "a terror to good conduct" rather than bad. Paul did "do what is good," but he did not "receive [Rome's] approval." He died, says tradition, as a flaming torch at one of Nero's parties. Yikes.

But Paul never had the chance to revise Romans 13. And so it has always been available to underwrite complacent Christian attitudes toward the state on the part of those who have no reason to fear it. No fear—not because they are good and innocent, and the state never harms the good and the innocent, but because they occupy a privileged position in American society, and thus all institutions of American society tend to benefit rather than harm them. In other words, Romans 13 read uncritically makes total sense if you are a white citizen of the middle or upper classes. It makes less sense if you are someone whose race and social position are not so favorable.

In the last several years, numerous videotaped incidents of police brutality, excessive force, and outright murder of black youths have exploded on the nation's consciousness. Trayvon Martin. Eric Garner. Tamir Rice. Michael Brown. These are just a few of the names of the most visible victims of excessive, unjust, or blatantly criminal use of police force. These incidents have helped fuel the influential Black Lives Matter movement and have provoked a nationwide debate on the police and their relation to black citizens in particular. Of course, polarization has followed, often along racial lines, though it is good news that many white allies have joined aggrieved family members, church leaders, and others from the nation's black communities.

The best analysis of the problem takes a long view. The perpetually second-class status of African Americans in American society has always been reflected in the use of state power against them. This includes but is not limited to the state power that is expressed by frontline police forces. It extends to every corner of government and every part of the criminal justice system. Both the first reconstruction after the Civil War and the second reconstruction of the Civil Rights movement have proven unable to break the pattern. It is simply part of the overall structural racism of American society; therefore, it is not dependent on any individual's personal racism or waywardness. It is more like the flow of the Mississippi—part of the cultural geography of American life.

Take just a cursory look at America in the Civil Rights years, and you will find ample evidence of police mistreatment of black people. Then look back at the lynching years of the early twentieth century. Then consider the post–Civil War years. And then the pre–Civil War years. And all the way back to the founding of the nation. The institutions of American state power at every level were set up by white people and were structured from the beginning in white racism and black subordination. Advances since 1865 have not been able to eliminate the effects of the original structuring in of white racism. Perhaps the most notable structural change has been the statutory federal commitment to side with African Americans against openly and viciously racist local and state-level authorities. This, sadly, has contributed to steady antigovernment feelings on the part of some, especially in the South.

Remember the difference between Paul and Jesus. Considered in this unfamiliar comparative context, one might say that in relation to the state, Jesus was black whereas Paul could at times at least pass as white. (See Reggie Williams, *Bonhoeffer's Black Jesus* [Baylor Press, 2014].) Jesus knew that he and his friends could be thrown on a cross at any moment and without any recourse, whereas Paul did not think that because it was not true for him. Just so, white people do not know in their bones that those nice men in their trim blue uniforms might just kill you unjustly, whereas African Americans certainly do know that. And until we white folks find ways to get beyond our privilege-induced myopia, we will never feel the urgency that we should to end police violence and unjust killings of black people.

It is tough as white people to hear that we just don't get it because our privileges blind us to realities beyond our experience, but it is much tougher to be a black parent afraid that your son or daughter won't make it home from a white section of town because they might be killed by a police officer. We who are privileged in this regard need to listen to those who are not, and we need to learn about best practices or at least best pro-posals for ending this scourge.

Every kind of practical step that makes sense is worth trying. The required use of body cameras by all police officers is at least one place to start; visibility and an end to deniability are certainly steps forward. The police have extraordinary power, as does the criminal justice system as a whole, and most police officers do not abuse their power. But like all other concentrations of power, this one needs checks and balances—such

as civilian oversight boards with real teeth and pros-
ecutors actually willing to prosecute law enforcers who
become lawbreakers.

The fear of social-contract theorists was that we
would create a state in order to secure our life, liberty,
and property but that it would end up overstepping its
bounds so that its mandate was negated rather than
achieved. Privileged people in any well-ordered society need only be concerned about occasional aberrations. African Americans and other people of color tell
us that aberrations are not occasional for them. Jesus
would understand. We should too. And then we should
change the situation.

11

SEX

Why We Never Stop Arguing about It

AMERICANS HAVE BEEN ARGUING ABOUT SEX FOR FIFTY years. The argument has taken different forms at different times, but in one sense it is always the same argument. It's about who is morally and legally allowed to have sex with whom and under what circumstances. More deeply, it is about how we know the answer to that question or who gets to make the rules.

The Supreme Court's *Obergefell v. Hodges* decision in 2015 legalizing same-sex marriage nationwide is the latest and probably the most intense episode in this ongoing argument about sex and the rules and laws that should govern it. For most progressive Christians and secular people, this decision was an overdue recognition of the dignity and equality of LGBT people and their relationships, and therefore a proper expression of both American and Christian values. For most conservative Christians, the decision marked a decisive rejection of biblical revelation, Christian (and American legal) tradition, and common sense.

In the aftermath of *Obergefell*, the divisions and anxieties continue. Christian progressives are anxious about conservatives rolling back marriage equality or preventing further advances in the fight for full LGBT rights. Christian conservatives are anxious about a country they fear has lost its moral compass. They also express considerable anxiety about threats to their liberty to teach and practice their religious faith—in homes, churches, schools, businesses, and beyond—as their conscience dictates.

Is there a healing word, or at least a clarifying one, that can be spoken into this maelstrom? Let's begin with an effort at offering some historical context.

The first wave of the sexual ethics argument began with the so-called sexual revolution of the 1960s. At its core, advocates of the sexual revolution wanted to free up Americans from what they believed were stifling rules and attitudes about sex, inherited from America's Christian past. These were rules and attitudes such as that sex belongs in (heterosexual) marriage alone, sex is primarily for making babies, babies need to be made only within the marital context, and the pleasures of sex are dangerous, perhaps immoral, and should be constrained.

The revolutionaries were not always actually revolutionary. Some simply wanted married couples to be able to enjoy sex more. Some wanted married couples to have access to reliable birth control—such as the new birth control pill—so that they could have sex without having to worry about getting pregnant. Of course, almost all Christians today, no matter how traditionalist, have no problem with the first of these goals, and most Christians have embraced the second goal as well. But the sexual revolution went further than this. Especially once the birth control pill was in wide circulation, the link between sex and baby-making weakened; consequently, so did the link between sex and marriage. One way to summarize this change was that people could have sex whenever they loved someone enough to want to do that. A more radical approach was to say that people could have sex whenever they felt like it, on their own terms and with their own motives.

Surely there never was a time in America when everyone or even nearly everyone adhered to the traditional sex-within-marriage standard. But during the 1960s, the standard essentially collapsed. Sex-for-love and sex-for-fun proliferated. So also, and despite the promise of birth control, did unplanned and unwanted pregnancies. So also, therefore, did the demand for abortion.

Meanwhile, beginning in the late 1960s and early 1970s, the gay rights movement emerged. Now traditional Christians were confronted with the more radical proposals that (a) there are people who are wired so as to desire romance and sex with members of the same rather than the opposite sex, and (b) sex might be morally permissible between such people, at least under some circumstances.

The arguments that emerged during the 1960s and 1970s have never really ended. In each case mentioned above, the liberalizing tendencies have broadly prevailed in American culture, and the law has changed in tandem and in response, quite recently in some cases. Legally, we live in a society where pretty much any adult can have sex with any other adult, married or single, and they can do so for whatever reasons they choose. If a woman gets pregnant, she can end her pregnancy with an abortion. Gay and lesbian people are now permitted to play by the same rules as anyone else in the sexual, relational, and marital game. Liberty and equality, two core American values, have prevailed over traditional Christian sexual morality. Despite very loud protests, there is no sign that these changes will be rolled back either in culture or law. Many Christians are angry, heartbroken, and anxious about some or all of the developments I have just outlined.

My own counsel to my fellow Christians is that it is best to avoid blanket rejection or acceptance of the entire range of social changes signaled by the term *sexual revolution*. Like everything else in human culture, these changes are a mixed bag.

Being able to view sex as a good and not shameful thing is legitimate progress. Freeing up married couples to be able to enjoy the sexual dimension of their relationship is progress. Allowing couples to have greater control over the number and timing of their children is progress. I believe that recognizing, accepting, and welcoming gay people into the joys and burdens of married life on the same terms as straight people is also progress. (For my take on this matter, see my book *Changing Our Mind* [Read the Spirit Books, 2014].)

I am much more ambivalent about other dimensions of the sexual revolution and what has happened since then. There were reasons for the traditional posture about sexuality that have not gone away. Sex really can and often does result in pregnancy, even with widely available birth control. Unwanted pregnancies often cannot be described as leading to a good outcome. A child born but unwanted and a child aborted because it's unwanted—these are both tragic outcomes.

Children also benefit from a secure and stable family life. If a husband doubts the parentage of his wife's child, this is a problem for the child. If a couple divorces because of sexual infidelity or the breakdown of a marriage for other reasons, this is a problem for the child. If a couple is attempting to manage multiple sexual relationships based on the surging interest in polyamory today, this is a problem for the child.

Social observers know that we have moved far beyond the soft liberalizing of sex-for-marriage to merely sex-for-love. Those who restrict sex to loving relationships are social conservatives in comparison to those who follow the sex-for-fun (and sex-for-exploitation) pattern that is increasingly taking hold, especially in the online social universe. One argument Christians have made for at least a love-based sexual ethic, if not a marital one, is that sex is about more than bodily pleasure or procreation. Sex has a natural tendency to bind lovers to one another—at least one possible meaning of "they become one flesh." Sex creates emotional connections because humans are neither animals that breed nor just autonomous wills that can deploy our bodies to have random sex for bodily pleasure alone. Instead, we are embodied selves who bring those selves into sexual encounters and do not leave such encounters unchanged. That, at least, is what we have said, and whether it will be disconfirmed in an era of routine casual sexual transactions is now being tested.

So if you are a Christian anxious that Americans, and in many cases American Christians, have given in to a chaotic liberalization of sexuality, you have good reason to be concerned. I have lived long enough and served long enough in pastoral ministry to have seen many promising young (and not-so-young) lives set back by sex-related mistakes underwritten by our newly liberalized sexual culture. I don't think we are called simply to accept a transactional or casual sexual ethic that has so much potential for harm, especially to those most vulnerable, including children. It is clear, however, that we are not finding much success simply commending the ways of the elders to our children and grandchildren on the basis of divine authority. We need to be able to marshal different kinds of evidence—including but not limited to biblical quotes—as to why those coming after us should tighten rather than loosen the connections, once again, between sex, love, marriage, and baby-making. As we do that, I believe we can relax our anxiety about the inclusion of the 3 to 5 percent of the population that is LGBT into a monogamous, marriage-based sexual ethic. That, at least, is the decision I (and many others) have now made.

12

ABORTION

The Sad Song That Never Ends

THERE IS NO LEGISLATIVE SOLUTION TO THE PROBLEM OF abortion. There is no president who can end abortion. There is no Supreme Court justice who will resolve the political conflict over abortion.

This is not just because we Americans, including we American Christians, have been shouting at each other about abortion for forty years with no end in sight. It is not just because the conflicting beliefs that people have about abortion are unlikely to change. It is not just because our polarized interest groups and political parties now gain support off of abortion. It is not just because the two "sides" on abortion are roughly balanced and appear likely to remain so.

Abortion is the sad song that never ends. It never ends because at one level it is an intractable human problem, visible in all times and cultures. It goes like this: Fertile heterosexual males and females are needy, passionate, sexual creatures who are drawn to each other and often end up having sex. They do so for all kinds of reasons—some good, some just okay, some terrible. When a fertile male and fertile female are "shooting with live bullets," sometimes the woman will get pregnant. This is true sometimes even when they are using birth control. The God-given power of mammalian reproduction is not easily denied.

Most every known society has attempted to create systems of social control to limit sexual contact between fertile men and women, in large part because of the procreative power of the mature human body. These have been remarkably comprehensive social systems. They have involved religious, political, legal, moral, communal, and familial efforts to train attitudes, impose constraints, inflame fears, and so on. Always they have involved efforts to limit private contact between sexually mature men and women outside the socially approved context for procreation—usually marriage.

Christian traditions have done this in their own way. The highest sources of religious authority (Bible, church) have been cited to ban sex between unmarried men and women. For centuries, and often still today, shaming efforts, especially of women who violate the ban, have been intense and harmful. The moral goodness of sex has been rejected altogether or, in recent decades, rejected until the wedding night. Churches have sought to support families in holding back the awesome power of sex for as long as possible, with various rates of success. Young couples have been pressed to marry as early and as quickly as possible. Babies born out of wedlock for centuries were labeled with an ugly epithet to complete the shaming of their "fallen" mothers. None of those efforts ever proved completely successful in holding back the tide. But since the 1960s, they have collapsed. Perhaps a nation as congenitally committed to personal freedom as America would always have been hard soil for efforts to keep the unmarried apart. But all kinds of factors have conspired at least since World War II to create a society whose conditions constitute a "perfect storm" for abortion: mass access to automobiles; coeducational schools; women's freedom to pursue professional ambitions; lack of parental oversight of dating relationships; liberalizing attitudes toward the morality of nonmarital sex, with all kinds of media encouraging further liberalization; the development, legalization, and mass distribution of contraception (combined with uneven use of it across the population); gradual delaying of the age of marriage due to the shift to a knowledge-based economy.

The historic 1973 decision of the Supreme Court in *Roe v. Wade* to legalize abortion was both result and cause of what has become a culture deeply dependent on abortion. (*Doe v. Bolton*, decided the same day, also matters. That decision rendered even Roe's late-term ban on abortion hopelessly weak.) The scheme to break the moral status of the fetus down along a trimester model was flimsy at the time and has collapsed since, and the legal rationale in a right to privacy never was all that persuasive. What the justices really should have said was something like this: "Given the powerful demand for abortion in our society, which has emerged based on an unforeseen convergence of social factors, any ban or serious limitation on women's access to abortion would be as unenforceable as Prohibition— and would be especially oppressive for women facing pregnancies that in their circumstances are personally disastrous. Regardless of one's personal religious or moral beliefs about abortion, an unenforceable law is a bad law, so we hereby grant access to abortion with the following limits . . ." If these limits had followed European models, they could have included a ban on non-emergency abortions after a certain number of weeks, such as sixteen.

Instead, the Court opened a societal wound that has never healed, despite several later efforts to reconsider the issue (such as the 1992 *Planned Parenthood v. Casey* case). Both prolife and prochoice activists have become more absolutist in the intervening years. State laws before 1973 had reflected and integrated a variety of considerations, including the circumstances of the pregnancy, the health of the fetus, and the stage of the pregnancy. Thoughtful Christians and others were able to discuss the pros and cons of various approaches to abortion law—three/two/one/no exceptions, timing, etc. And positions on abortion were not locked into a partisan or liberal/conservative binary. But increasingly in the decades after 1973, it was all or nothing— no limits on abortion ever, for any reason, and no moral pressure to consider options, versus no access to abortion ever, for any reason, in any circumstance. The extremes prevailed, reinforcing each other, often with competing horror stories. Here's the twenty-four-week-old fetus that barely survived a late-term abortion and now lives. There's the fragile eleven-year-old rape victim who may die carrying her legally enforced pregnancy to term. The idea that we might be able to create a legal framework in which we can agree that both of those rare situations must never happen has proved to be beyond us. Meanwhile, nonemergency, nonexceptional abortions go on and on and on, because the social circumstances that create them remain unchanged, if not worsened.

What is an anxious Christian to do about all this? Understanding the universal human and then particularly American cultural factors that lie behind the demand for abortion should certainly help. Absent a social revolution, the effort to reduce abortion on the demand side is the only meaningful path forward. This involves creating subcultures of resistance to a culture dependent on abortion. This is the one thing the churches can do that is meaningful. To do this involves teaching sexual restraint without shame, teaching best practices for birth control when sexual restraint has reached its limit, and creating family and church communities that can support couples who face unwanted pregnancies and are seeking alternatives to abortion.

There are times when policies really are pretty extreme and need to be addressed. Having actually held dead eighteen-week-old fetuses in my hands on two particularly sad days of my life, I think it is a travesty that abortion is permitted in nonemergency circumstances as late as that. But I would also strongly oppose any attempts to start banning abortion for preteens who have been raped or are victims of incest. Probably the basic structure of abortion law in the United States will change little, though there is the outside chance that the matter will be sent back to the individual states, which would then impose a patchwork quilt of laws like those that existed prior to 1973. This would reconfigure the circumstances faced by women who desire to end their pregnancies, and in many cases, it would increase their hardship. But this outcome, which many in the prolife movement would consider a huge achievement, would do nothing to change the convergent social forces that have gotten us where we are. So I do not think it should be our focus. Instead, we must address the prevention side, the demand side, and we must take the side of young women who need deep personal and systemic help to avoid having to face that miserable drive to the abortion clinic.

13

ALIENS

About Who Belongs Here and Who Doesn't

THE IMMIGRATION ISSUE NEVER SEEMS TO GO AWAY. NOR does it show any signs of being resolved. It resurfaces in often ugly ways with every election campaign. And, like almost everything else that matters, it is now subject to culture-war divisions. Even so, clear and reasonably nonideological Christian thinking is possible, leading to some appropriately faithful Christian actions.

Some facts that we all ought to be able to agree on include the following: The nation-state system has not existed forever, but it exists now and shows no signs of going away. Nation-states now function as the primary way to organize large human communities, establish citizenship status for individuals, offer security and human rights protections, and set recognized boundaries between countries. The actual borders between countries are the product of a variety of factors. There is nothing absolute about them, and they can change over time. But at any given moment, they play a significant role in the real world. Every nation has laws related to border protection, border crossing, immigration, and emigration. Nations have a legitimate interest in screening those attempting to cross into their territory. They have an even more serious interest in deciding who may reside within their borders temporarily or permanently and in establishing a clear legal status for everyone. Nations establish immigration and border-security laws and enforcement mechanisms to achieve these goals.

For many reasons, including those described in the first chapter, the United States has long been an attractive destination for people from other nations to visit, to reside in for a while, or to join as citizens. It is an economic, cultural, and political magnet, and by comparison with many nations in the world, the life we enjoy here is infinitely more appealing. Moreover, the vast economic engine of the United States regularly draws workers here, whether legally or illegally, temporarily or permanently, simply according to the iron laws of capitalism. The United States has regularly welcomed temporary and permanent emigrants from other countries, often for economic reasons but sometimes as an expression of a periodic national impulse to serve as a place of refuge for those who need or want to come here.

The length and porousness especially of our southern border, combined with the desperate desire of many people to our south to come to the United States, has created the conditions for a massive inflow of immigrants who violate U.S. law in order to cross our border or to stay after a visa has expired. Typical estimates place the number of these undocumented immigrants at around eleven million. Most but not all are Latin Americans, which means that Spanish is their primary language and Christianity is their predominant religion. Most end up working in the shadows of an underground economy that in many cases depends on their labor. There is no evidence that undocumented immigrants in any large number create significant social problems, participate in crime, harm American citizens, cost U.S. taxpayers money, or materially change U.S. culture. Precisely because they know they are here illegally and are vulnerable to deportation, they tend to stay in the shadows and out of trouble.

As a policy matter, there are two fundamental questions related to illegal immigration as it pertains to our southern border. First, if we are determined to enforce our often-violated immigration laws, what steps must we take to do so? Second, what do we do with the eleven million human beings who are already here?

There is no reason why these questions should become fodder for culture warriors. Border security and immigration-law enforcement do not bear any obvious resemblance to issues such as same-sex marriage or abortion. Tragically, however, some politicians and some Americans have turned immigration into a kind of culture-war issue anyway. To do so, they have exaggerated the low threat to Americans posed by illegal immigrants. Americans have been fortunate that we have absorbed eleven million illegal immigrants into our society without having substantial problems with them. It could have turned out differently, and it could turn out differently in the future. With determined terrorists seeking to harm us, a porous border is a really bad idea. But these eleven million are not terrorists of any variety. They are no threat. But most do not want to go back to their home countries, and they resist deportation efforts with every fiber of their being.

The logical and reasonably humane solution has been placed before the U.S. Congress several times since the George W. Bush administration. It includes tightening border security dramatically and providing a mechanism to identify, process, and finally welcome the noncriminal 99.9 percent of the current undocumented immigrant population. Most versions of the latter plan include some kind of fine for having broken immigration law, a period of waiting for the lengthy process that will be required to clear this backlog of cases, a requirement of a working knowledge of English and American civics, and a path to citizenship or at least permanent residence.

Conservatives tend to be enthusiastic about the border security part and not about the naturalization process. Liberals tend to be enthusiastic about the latter rather than the former. In my view, both parts are absolutely essential, at least in the real world that we live in.

This both/and approach of comprehensive immigration reform remains the best option for Christians. This challenges conservative Christians to soften their hearts and welcome the strangers who would make it through the arduous naturalization process that lies ahead. But it also challenges progressive Christians to take concerns about border security and immigration law seriously.

I happen to know many progressive Christians so inspired by Jesus' transcendent vision of the kingdom of God and by broader biblical principles that they are impatient with all this talk of border security. After all, is our God really someone who sees or cares about national borders, lines on an invisible map that we humans have drawn over God's good creation? What about the intrinsic dignity of every person and Christ's call that we love our neighbors as ourselves? Isn't our true citizenship in heaven anyway? Why should we care about the enforcement of U.S. immigration law?

These are penetrating and important questions. As with other problems that we face in the world today, they raise the agonizing issue of how to integrate the stringent demands of Christian discipleship, and of a faith that is about a transformed world, with the requirements of nation-states and the complexities of a world not yet transformed. Navigating this intersection often demands of us some kind of compromise, some effort to make progress toward, or to approximate, kingdom-of-God values, even if we cannot achieve them in their fullness.

On this particular issue, I think that approximation looks like the type of comprehensive immigration reform that finds a way to welcome most of the eleven million who are here but also finds a way to secure our borders. One day, all borders will drop away. But we have not yet reached that day.

Chapter 14

GUNS

Our Most Obvious Sickness

WHICH PARTICULAR RECENT U.S. GUN MASSACRE AFFECTED you the most? Was it Sandy Hook, where a disturbed young man murdered twenty six- and seven-year-olds and six adults? Was it Orlando? San Bernadino? Virginia Tech? Fort Hood? Columbine? Can you keep track of them anymore? Can you tell which particular crazy/aggrieved/failed dude who wanted to end his miserable little life in a blaze of gunfire brought which particular military-grade killing arsenal to murder which particular group of innocent people in which particular little town on the worst day that town would ever know—to be followed by 24/7 news coverage, police officials earnestly going on TV reconstructing every detail of the crime, stuffed animals and flowers at the killing/pilgrimage site, politicians calling for prayer and half of them calling for action that never comes, the stupid circular arguments in the media, (ex)friends cursing each other on Facebook as they argue, over and over and over again?

If you have made it this far, dear anxious Christian friend, you will know that on many issues I am the soul of sweet reason and patient dialogue. (Right?) But on this issue, my sweetness, reason, and patience have now left me. Our beloved country is wonderful in many respects, troubled in others, but on no other issue do we seem as completely out of our minds as on this one. Our 11,000 annual deaths by gunfire are a public health crisis, an international spectacle, a daily source of grief for dozens of families, a national security issue, and an atrocious public policy failure. And our paralysis, our inability to do anything to address this problem, is one of the greatest examples of national dysfunction that we currently see.

The United States has a firearm-related death rate of 10.64 per 100,000 people (2013). That puts us in the ballpark with Argentina (9.63), Mexico (15.37), Panama (15.86), South Africa (13.61), and Uruguay (15.36). Meanwhile, among what we would normally consider peer nations, consider these numbers.

Australia: 0.93
Canada: 2.22
France: 2.83
Germany: 1.01
New Zealand: 1.07

Netherlands: 0.58
United Kingdom: 0.23*

The United States has what amounts to a developing-country profile when it comes to gun deaths. Other nations, wracked by civil war, guerrilla violence, the drug trade, the aftermath of tyranny, corrupt police forces, and weak governing institutions, have far better reasons than we do to suffer these kinds of gun violence numbers. But our peer nations—actually, let's face it, we think of ourselves as so good and so advanced that we are without peer—are so far ahead of us on gun safety that there is no real comparison. It's embarrassing—and disastrous.

There are many different ways of understanding the cultural and political forces that have gotten us here. One factor is a kind of confidence in violence in general, and the gun in particular, that goes back to colonial days. Guns helped defeat the Native Americans from our earliest settlements. Guns helped defeat the British. Guns went west as Americans did. Guns became a beloved part of many American homes. Narrating and renarrating these formative experiences became and to some extent still remains a major feature of American leisure-time entertainment. All these can be seen as helping to create a gun culture here that is different from many peer nations.

*"List of countries by Firearm-Related Death Rate," *Wikipedia*, https://en.Wikipedia.org/wiki/List_of_countries_by_firearm -related_death_rate.

One particular feature of the Wild West experience/ myth has been especially important. In the typical Western, the forces of official law and order are weak. Everyone, especially every man, seems to be armed, and every man needs to be prepared to use his weapon to defend himself and his family. And sometimes the decent people of a community must band together collectively to defeat outlaws who are far too much for the lone sheriff to handle.

Remember that both Romans 13 and the social-contract theory envision a delegating of violence (either from above or below) from the individual to the state to guard everyone against threats to life and property. If the forces of law and order are both trustworthy and strong, then no individual has to constitute his own security force. He can call the police. And with foreign threats, the president can call out the military. One of the perennial challenges of human community is moving from vigilantism and the war of all against all to a peaceful, well-ordered society that includes a centralized power with sufficient strength (and threat thereof) that citizens do not have to function as their own police force.

In addition, Americans were (and some still are) afraid about what would happen if the government they set up became a tyranny. Many gun advocates passionately defend gun rights precisely on this point. If somehow a Hitler were to ascend to power in the United States, they argue, Americans could defend themselves house to house with the arsenals they have acquired for this purpose.

Of course, when one considers the hardware and skills of a trained U.S. soldier and then lays these alongside Harry the Homeowner with his gun or three, there really is no comparison. Advances in military weaponry and training have just gone too far for civilian self-defense to be a realistic possibility. As for the much-debated Second Amendment, here is a case where poor wording and changed circumstances render the interpretation of this critical sentence immensely difficult. What the framers intended by "the right of the people to keep and bear arms," especially as it follows after "a well-regulated Militia, being necessary to the security of a free state," is not entirely clear. But it seems most likely to have meant this: in a context in which the fragile young America was a long way from having a large, well-equipped standing army, and in which the gap in weaponry between the average soldier and the average homeowner was much smaller than it is today, a well-armed, readily mobilized civilian militia was both possible and necessary. But now, more than two hundred years later, interpreting the Second Amendment in a way that allows pretty much everyone to buy all kinds of guns is looking like a really bad idea.

What if we are discovering that we are simply not a healthy enough society to allow ourselves essentially unregulated access to all these guns? Perhaps we could imagine a society of sober, sane, disciplined, moral, careful gun owners, those doughty militiamen of yore. Of course, that is what many gun owners are. But surely we have seen, with our 11,000 annual gun deaths, that not all of us are sober, sane, disciplined, moral, and careful. Too many people with access to a gun are impaired, insane, undisciplined, immoral, and careless. They leave guns around for toddlers or troubled adolescents to get their hands on. They are among our vast substance-abusing population. They are angry and use their guns to harm themselves or others. They are pathological and decide to shoot up movie theaters. Or they are suicidal *and* pathological and want to imitate other recent heroes by staging a great drama in which they kill children and then die in the end by their own hand. Or, now, they are religiously motivated terrorists who exploit our lax gun laws to do to us what their friends did to Paris.

That is where we are. Rational people, when they find that a practice is not working out as intended, change that practice. But the more Americans get killed by guns, the more Americans buy guns in order to protect themselves against the guns that were previously available because Americans wanted to ensure that they would not get killed by guns. Guns are intended to secure us; they are making us less secure. And this ought to make us anxious.

What are we to do? We can pass commonsense gun safety laws that include universal background checks (currently no more than 60 percent of actual gun sales involve such checks); banning domestic abusers from retaining or buying guns; requiring "smart guns" only usable by their (screened) owner; blocking sales of semi-automatic, military-grade weapons; reversing "stand your ground" laws; implementing microstamping of ammunition so that guns used in crimes can be traced; improving mental-health screening for gun purchasers; and ending the negligence-related immunity enjoyed by gun manufacturers and sellers. We might start by allowing government research on all these matters, research blocked now by the gun lobbyists who donate so heavily to Congress.

More deeply, some of the premises of our gun culture need to be challenged. The most dangerous of these is that having three hundred million guns in civilian hands makes us safer. If it was ever true, it is not now so. Anxious Christians, let's end this gun culture as soon as we can.

Chapter 15

MONEY

Beyond Competitive Selfishness

IN MOST ELECTION YEARS, MOST ARGUMENTS AMONG POLITical parties and their leaders have to do with money. You know—greenbacks, simoleons, cash, taxes, welfare, inequality, regulation, interest rates, jobs, stocks. Talk about polarization. Arguments over economic questions are the background noise of American politics. After a while they become so predictable you pretty much want to hit snooze as soon as the politicians start with their talking points. And Christians tend to track along with the arguments of their ideological favorites, which is boring, uncreative, and unilluminating.

One somewhat fresher way to enter the conversation is to draw a distinction between two ways of looking at the economic life of any society: competitive and cooperative.

The competitive model sees human beings as ineluctably competing against each other for all the good things of material life: employment, good wages, promotions, adequate housing, economic security, a reliable pot of money for old age. If I get this job, twenty others will not. If you get promoted to the one open position, I will not. If your age cohort gets its economic security met by a generous retirement system, my cohort will have fewer resources going our way. I can afford a house in this neighborhood, but you cannot. Even if you could pay for it, I could bid higher so that only one of us could live here. If Walmart comes to town, I can buy cheap stuff. But it will drive small shops out of business. If Amazon sells cheaper books than the local Barnes & Noble, the bookstore will lose sales and may go out of business. Win/lose, win/lose, win/lose. It is hard to deny the relentlessly competitive, win/lose nature of economic life. Many individual and corporate losers pile up by the side of the road because, after all, not everyone can win.

Of course, the counter to this tale of relentless competition has been in circulation since Adam Smith and his notion of the "invisible hand" of the market. He argued that a capitalist economy cunningly harnesses human competitiveness in a way that advances the self-interest of all effective competitors and the common good of the society as a whole.

You want to run the most prosperous auto repair shop in town. I want to make as much money as I can with the auto repair skills that I have developed. She wants to drive a car that runs reliably so that she can get to work to succeed at her job, where her employer wants to run the best consulting firm in the area, which involves compensating her for her skills at a high level. Every economic agent is simultaneously buyer and seller, seeking economic advancement as they define it, thrown into a strange kind of cooperation with others, all of us without any particular will to cooperate. Day after day we each pursue our self-interest, which ends up advancing all of us. I am writing at Barnes & Noble because I am pursuing my professional and financial goals. The workers here are earning their (rather pitiful) pay as they pursue their goals. The authors of all the books here found it worth their while to publish, as did the publishers who produced them, and for now Barnes & Noble does well enough to provide a decent return to those who own shares in the company.

Most political arguments in capitalist economies concern tweaks to the functioning of the economy. These include issues ranging from preparing workers for gainful employment, to regulating market exchanges and business activity, to taxing economic income and profits in order to fund government activities agreed on by political representatives.

The problem with a purely competitive paradigm, or even the somewhat modified competitive paradigm just described, is that it cannot really account for any motive in personal, business, or societal economic decisions other than self-interest. Those of us schooled on a pure competition paradigm are trained to view all economic and policy decisions purely from a selfish perspective. What is best for me? What will benefit my firm? What will likely advance the interests of those I love? So deeply trained in mass selfishness, we hardly notice it after a while—perhaps until somebody's selfishness becomes so blatant that it crosses our (very limited) legal boundaries and becomes criminal (see Bernie Madoff, for example). Then we send that one person off to jail and go back to business. But otherwise we systematically keep pursuing our self-interest while blinding ourselves to its victims.

The tendency of capitalist economies to breed selfishness has been noticed and protested since the beginning of modern capitalism. An early form of protest was to make moral appeals, asking the most powerful actors in capitalist economies to be more humane and less selfish—by, for example, improving working conditions, increasing pay, and decreasing hours. These almost always failed miserably; systemic competitive selfishness was already in capitalism's bloodstream.

Activists and politicians, including many Christians, eventually concluded that moral persuasion would never be enough. Pretty much all aspects of economic-related activity would need to be regulated for the well-being of the weakest and most vulnerable. And the massive raw power of the largest economic actors, such as major corporations, needed the most careful regulating by the only power big enough to check their activities—the federal government. Meanwhile a decent social safety net would need to be created to cushion the blows of capitalism for those who could not compete, or could not compete any longer, in the economy. And thus was born regulated capitalism, or what was sometimes called "the mixed economy." In my view, most of the regulations and reforms instituted since the Progressive Era have been needed to ensure minimal human well-being and basic rights, and most have not slowed down the American economy in any significant way.

The Catholic Church has developed a rich body of teachings about economic ethics over the last 125 years, as have many Protestant traditions. These teachings began with a strong effort to retrain all economic participants in supposedly Christian societies to think of themselves as involved in a cooperative endeavor in which no one wins unless everyone wins. Still today, Christian social ethics remains one of the strongest voices urging a "common good" approach to economic life rather than a strictly competitive model. In making this argument, the Catholic Church especially draws on an ancient way of looking at the world, one that preceded the birth of capitalism and is in fact embedded in the New Testament in texts like 1 Corinthians 12. There Paul offers an image of the Christian community as a body, with many members but one purpose and all of them deeply interconnected. "If one member suffers, all suffer together with it" (1 Cor. 12:26). For centuries in the era of Christendom, Christians were taught to view entire communities as organic cooperative entities, as a kind of social body of Christ, with everyone playing a part, everyone's part honored and respected, and everyone concerned for the well-being of the whole and not just themselves.

No one talks about society or economic life like that today—except, perhaps, for Catholics. But maybe this is at least one principle that anxious Christians today can make our own. What if we thought of every one of the 320 million Americans (not to mention the rest of the world) as part of one body? What if our economic vision asked about the well-being especially of the weakest and most vulnerable members of this body— so that the quality of not only my kids' school matters but the schools of the poorest kids in town matter? So that not only having great highways accessible from my suburb matters, but having a great mass transit system for those who don't have cars matters? So that not only my Social Security benefits matter, but the child care available to working single mothers matters? So that not only the health benefits package I get from work matters, but also the Medicaid available to the poorest and the Obamacare available to the next to poorest matters? So that not only getting "everyday low prices" matters, but also whether the people who serve me at Walmart, Chili's, and Barnes & Noble make enough money to support themselves? This is not all there is to say about money. But it's a start.

16

CLIMATE

The Ultimate Rorschach Test?

When newspapers reported in late January 2016 that NASA and NOAA (the National Oceanic and Atmospheric Administration) had declared 2015 to be the hottest year in recorded history, what did Americans see in those headlines? The authoritative warnings of government scientists doing the jobs we are paying them to do? The exaggerated claims of ideologically driven liberals getting ahead of the science, fostering alarmism, and snagging more money for themselves? Which is it? What do we see? Why do we see what we think we see? Climate, of all current issues, seems like the ultimate Rorschach test. What we see depends very much on what we bring to the seeing.

More than with other topics in this book, here I will be openly autobiographical. I want to say as clearly as possible what I bring to the seeing process when it comes to climate science and policy. Maybe this can help the anxious Christian reader to do the same.

I grew up in a northern Virginia household led by an MIT-trained chemical engineer. During most of my growing-up years, my father worked as an energy and environmental policy analyst for the Congressional Research Service (CRS) of the Library of Congress. This relatively unknown outfit is one of the federal government's hidden gems. Here is a collection of scholarly specialists who are required to offer well-researched, evenhanded, dispassionate briefings to members of Congress and their staffs. Any hint of bias or partisanship would destroy their credibility and probably threaten the very existence of this office.

My father is a hard-headed scientist who undertook research and offered briefings that contributed to the first major round of environmental legislation of the 1960s and 1970s: the Clean Air Act, the Clean Water Act, and so on. He was never really an environmentalist; that movement's perspectives were simply part of the overall data picture that he analyzed. But Dad did say, in his careful way, that it had become abundantly clear by the 1960s that since the Industrial Revolution, human beings had developed the capacity to do substantial damage to the creation—and *were* doing substantial damage. Nature (God's creation) had been designed with extraordinary resilience in the face of inevitable ecological impacts, but this resilience is not infinite. No living organism has infinite resilience. The strongest, healthiest human body has considerable resilience, but the human person inhabiting that body can make decisions that threaten and finally destroy his or her own bodily health. The same thing was proving true in relation to the creation as a whole.

One key role of natural scientists is to monitor the status of ecological resilience. They are trained to take the earth's temperature. They examine the health of the oceans and rivers, the lakes and streams, the forests and savannahs, the beaches and deserts. They pay attention to the living and the dying of the millions of species of plants and animals that share our planet with us. Their warnings, along with the observations of amateur naturalists of all types as well as regular folks who know dirty drinking water and polluted air when they see it, helped stir humanity all across the world to take seriously the damages we were already doing to the creation. And they taught us to see that what we do to "the creation," we do to other creatures. And what we do to other creatures, we eventually do to ourselves. They emphasized the interconnectedness of all life on earth, not because of some mystic theory, but because it is what their data showed them. And so in the 1960s and 1970s, the U.S. government developed a policy response to better take care of our land, our seas, our air, and ourselves. My father was part of that. He was rightly proud of that work. And it gave him confidence that we could mobilize ourselves to take collective action again in the future if it might be needed.

Beginning in the 1980s, those scientists specializing in monitoring local, regional, and global climate began to coalesce around the conclusion that the overall temperature of the atmosphere was rising consistently. This had not happened before in the history of temperature monitoring. Some worked to discover the most important causes of what became known as global warming. Others worked to develop models of what the likely impacts would be of continued warming at various levels. Still others began thinking about what became known as climate mitigation and climate adaptation—that is, what human beings can do to slow or reverse the trend, and to the extent we cannot succeed in slowing or reversing the trend, what we will need to do to adapt to it.

The issue began to be viewed with sufficient seriousness that the United Nations established a massive research apparatus to investigate these questions. That became known as the Intergovernmental Panel on Climate Change (IPCC), and it has been reporting its results every six or seven years for more than twenty-five years. I have read several of the massive IPCC reports (all are publicly available), and they certainly give every evidence of reflecting an impressive body of scientific research. Scientists I know who have been involved with IPCC say that the work is done at the highest level possible and that the findings are stated in muted rather than alarmist terms. This happens, in part, because government officials ultimately have to approve IPCC documents, and some of them (such as those representing the oil-exporting states) have an economic interest in reporting cautiously on the extent and dangers of climate change.

My father, now well into his retirement, tends to be cautious about climate science. He is concerned that some of the most vocal scientific voices on climate change have gone beyond the evidence as we now have it because they are convinced of the deep seriousness of the overall trajectory. The problem is this: if the near-worst or worst estimates of the impact of global warming are right, then human beings have to act now—when the evidence of climate change and its negative impacts is smaller than it one day will be—to prevent full-on disaster later. But human inertia, disbelief, and self-interest make it very difficult for people to act aggressively to address a problem that does not present itself to most of them as imminent or pressing.

But the situation is even worse than this. In 2006, when I drafted an evangelical declaration on climate change, an impressive array of conservative evangelicals were willing to sign off on a statement that said (1) climate change is real; (2) its impacts will be serious, beginning with the poor and regions of the world most economically and ecologically vulnerable; (3) Christian moral convictions demand a response; and (4) the need to act now is urgent, with everyone having a role to play. This document came out at a time when there was pretty strong bipartisan support for substantial climate change legislation in Congress.*

But after 2008 the issue became a partisan one. Republicans en masse began rejecting the claims represented in our declaration, all the way down to the very first one about the basic reality of climate change. Now the whole climate-change thing was a hoax on the American public being dreamed up by leftists, statists,

---

*"Climate Change: An Evangelical Call to Action," http://creation care.org/climate-realists-energy-optimists/evangelical-climate -initiative.

Norwegian socialists, grant-hungry scientists, faux evangelicals, you name it. And as I write during an election cycle, all major GOP presidential candidates express near-total indifference to the climate change issue. Every action that President Obama has taken to address climate change in the global or domestic policy arenas has been met by a wall of Republican opposition. And because most white evangelicals are Republicans, most treat climate change in about the same way.

There are some pretty deep theological reasons why many Christians just can't take climate change seriously. For some, their God is so big and their humanity so small that they simply cannot accept that humanity has this kind of climate-altering power or that a sovereign God would allow it. Some are still working from a theology of human dominion over creation that appears to authorize a rather libertine approach to the creation—we want it, we take it, we use it, it's ours. A sense of mission focused exclusively on the eternal salvation of human souls rather than anything much that happens here contributes to a kind of constitutional indifference to human affairs. An overall distrust of modern science, especially natural science, remains a residue of the evolution fights that have never really gone away since Darwin. And of course, once the issue became a partisan one, with the Democrats associated with concern for climate and the Republicans resolutely opposed, the door closed even more tightly for many Christians identified with the Republicans.

I grieve that so many of my anxious Christian friends have gotten themselves into this posture in relation to what the vast majority of climate scientists are telling us about the distress of the natural world. I plead with them (you?) to ask whether they really believe that our sovereign God wouldn't let us do this kind of damage to the earth and to other humans. The next time they go to the hospital for diagnosis and treatment, I plead with them to ask whether they are really as skeptical of modern natural science as they sound on this issue. I ask whether they really believe that a scientific community that fifty years ago rightly analyzed the damage we were doing to the water we drink and the air we breathe has now utterly lost all credibility.

In most of these chapters, I have sought to calm the anxieties of American Christians. In this case, I seek to inflame them. Just as we addressed toxic air and water, we can address global warming and its consequences. But American Christians can't keep dragging their feet about it.

17

WAR

Have We Had Enough Yet?

AMERICANS HAVE A PRETTY CONFLICTED ATTITUDE ABOUT war, and the situation is dynamic and unsettled. Much will be determined by the direction our country takes in the next few years, as well as by international events over which we have little control. Christians need to think seriously and in fresh ways about these issues right now, grounded in our faith and not giving in to fear and anxiety.

It is fair to say that of all current Western nations, ours is the most likely to use military force. The forms of that use of force vary, ranging from drone strikes to the insertion of "special operators" to clandestine CIA missions to announced troop deployments. At the time of this writing, the country is debating which approach is best to deal with the threat of the radical Islamist group ISIS in Iraq, Syria, Libya, and elsewhere. And ISIS is only the latest national-security threat to which we are responding with military force. Our use of military force seems to have been more or less constant since World War II.

Almost no living American has any memory of a time when the United States was not on a war footing of some sort. With the exception of a very brief window after the collapse of the Soviet Union in 1991, our country has been in a constant state of war since the Pearl Harbor attack of December 7, 1941. That's seventy-five years!

From 1941 to 1945 we were, of course, engaged in a multifront war against Nazi Germany, Imperial Japan, and their allies. After we won World War II, we went immediately into a Cold War with the Soviet Union. After the Soviet Union exploded its first atomic bomb in 1949, following our actual use of atomic weapons at the end of World War II, this Cold War became a showdown involving the daily risk of the use of weapons of mass destruction. For over forty years, the dreams and nightmares of people the world over were inhabited by the threat of nuclear annihilation.

When the Communist regimes of the Eastern Bloc collapsed and then the Soviet Union stunningly collapsed as well, it seemed that this global tension would finally ease and that we might know something like peace. But in 1993 came the first attack on the World Trade Center by radicalized Muslims, then the September 11 attacks orchestrated by Osama bin Laden and al-Qaeda, wars in Afghanistan and Iraq, and now ISIS.

In this seventy-five-year period of war, the character of our country, and certainly of our government, has changed. A massive military and security apparatus, along with the industrial base that services it, is now a permanent feature of our national life and is active all over the world. We never demobilize. We never get off of a war footing. It is a commonplace observation that war and democracy are an uneasy mix. Clearly, since World War II, the power of the presidency and the executive branch has grown in relation to Congress and the courts, at least in the security arena. The president as commander-in-chief is assumed to have the authority to order various kinds of military actions, in many cases without any congressional authorization. When President George W. Bush and Vice President Dick Cheney authorized torture after 9/11, oversight processes were too weak to do much to stop them, at least for the first several years of abuse. The struggle of Congress even to be able to release a heavily censored executive summary of a secret report on what happened in the CIA "enhanced interrogation" campaign signals severe limits on democratic accountability for our (many) clandestine services.

It is hard to remember that there was a time when the United States was reluctant to engage in military actions. Though we dabbled in imperialism in the late nineteenth and early twentieth centuries (as in the Philippines), we were somewhat late to that game and never got into it wholeheartedly. We had to be dragged into World War I, and it was only the stupendous miscalculations of Japan and Nazi Germany that got us into World War II in December 1941.

We had leaders who knew quite well and were concerned about what would happen if we moved to a permanent war footing. One of these was the iconic general, and then president, Dwight Eisenhower, who at the end of his presidency in 1960 warned against a permanent "military-industrial complex" taking root in America. What a surprising and prophetic speech that was! And widely ignored, at least in retrospect.

Two formative wars early in our history still help shape our national consciousness, and in ways that probably weaken our resistance to war. Our miraculous success in defeating imperial Great Britain during the Revolutionary War stands at the very origins of our national history. Various lessons can be drawn from the conflict, but surely it has helped shape our national ethos in a way different from nations like, say, Canada and Australia. We were born in blood and violence, and all those guns and muskets won us our freedom. This we celebrate every July 4, always reinforcing the links between American identity, freedom, and military force.

Our memory of the Civil War, despite its being a horrific slaughterhouse, also reinforces tendencies toward what might fairly be called U.S. militarism. Those who identify with the North can connect war and violence with victory and moral good, notably freedom for slaves and the preservation of the Union. Those who identify with the South have often shown a tendency to connect that war with the "lost cause" of preserving the Southern way of life, "gone with the wind" after the defeat and the subsequent impositions of Reconstruction. It is a natural tendency for people to want to honor those who "made the ultimate sacrifice" in war, and this is perhaps accentuated in Southern memory by the national moral rejection of the Southern cause. The fact that the United States always "wins" played a major role, for a long while at least, in shaping national attitudes toward war. A Northerner, at least, could once point to an unbroken string of American military successes. Surely this reinforced complacency about the use of armed force by the United States. But ever since Vietnam, the record has been much more mixed. The casualties have been high, both in visible and subtle ways. We have gotten bogged down in countries, Iraq and Afghanistan, from which we cannot seem to extricate ourselves. And the hydra-headed threat of radical Islam seems impervious to our frantic efforts. If we take out a key leader over here, another one pops up over there. If we decapitate al-Qaeda, here comes ISIS, seemingly even more ruthless, more deadly, more powerful. It's whack-a-mole, and it never stops.

What are Christians who are also Americans supposed to make of all this? Is it as simple as saying that Jesus taught peace and nonviolence, so we must reject the entire war-making enterprise, at least in terms of our own personal participation in it? Or is it as simple as saying that nations have to defend themselves and their people and so we just need to keep doing what we are doing, maybe even more aggressively?

Here is my best, most honest short answer. Nations will seek their own security. National leaders will (and should) feel a strong obligation to protect their citizens from being killed or maimed by terrorists or enemy countries. Citizens should and often do feel a strong desire to protect not only themselves and their families but also other citizens and their families. Part of being a community is caring about people with whom you share life in that community.

Nations have many tools in their security toolbox, however. Most of these tools are nonviolent, including diplomatic and economic resources. Those Americans who are also Christian should be strong advocates for the fullest possible use of every nonviolent tool available to those we entrust with government and security leadership. Because of the teaching and example of Jesus, we should begin with a default resistance to war (and quasi-war), and we should seek to communicate that resistance to those who represent us in government. We should name and resist what has become a default tendency to resort to violence early and often. We should also name and resist what has become a deep tendency in our national life to valorize war and warriors as central to our national character and identity. And we need to resist any further tendency to weaken moral and constitutional limits on the waging of war by our country—such as becoming nonchalant about civilian casualties, ever again resorting to torture, or enhancing the power of the president to wage war.

Many American Christians are understandably anxious about terrorism and the threat of ISIS. That's because we do not want to die. We do not want our loved ones to die. We want to be safe when we get on an airplane, go to work, or go out to eat. All of this makes total sense. It helps to remember that a response to our fear in the form of more violence initiated by our country may have a superficial satisfaction but may make us less safe in the long run. And it also helps to remember that for a Christian, neither fear nor death is allowed to be our ultimate motivator. We are committed to following Jesus the best way we can in our stubbornly sinful world.

Chapter 18

EXECUTIONS

A Strange Anachronism

ABOUT THIRTY TIMES A YEAR, STATE OFFICIALS IN OUR country take one of the thousands of prisoners under their care on a journey toward death. As calmly, orderly, and clinically as possible, they inject poison into the veins of their prisoner in order to kill him (or her). And then death comes.

A proverbial alien visiting from another planet would not be able to discern any logical reason why this or that particular prisoner on this or that particular night is selected to be killed. The United States is a large country, but only a small number of states actually execute prisoners anymore, and closer examination also shows that there is inconsistency within particular states. Our alien would discover that it is certainly not as simple as the application of a uniform punishment for a particular crime. There were over sixteen thousand murders in the United States in 2013, but that year only thirty-nine people were executed for the crime of murder, and the numbers have been similar for the last several years. That's a 0.24 percent execution rate.*

So who gets executed? A very small, almost arbitrary slice of those convicted of murder in our violent society. Mainly those who live in a few southern and southwestern states—such as Texas, Virginia, Oklahoma, and Georgia—known for their combination of religious zeal and support for the death penalty. Disproportionately, those who are black. Disproportionately, those who are poor. Disproportionately, those who kill white people. Disproportionately, those who did not have strong legal representation.

Our alien observer might ask this question: what is gained by the continued existence of the death penalty as it is so occasionally, randomly, and discriminatorily practiced? An honest answer that makes much sense is hard to come by. It cannot be that executing fewer than one-quarter of 1 percent of all murderers, and only in a small number of states, serves any consistent or broad public purpose. Those contemplating killing someone do not really have to worry that they will be killed by the state in response, as the odds are just too low, like getting hit by lightning. Citizens worried about violent crime cannot rationally take comfort in the idea that potential murderers will be deterred from doing so

---

*The best source for death penalty information is the website of the Death Penalty Information Center: http://www.deathpenaltyinfo .org.

because of the odd possibility of a random execution happening to them. Those motivated by a strong sense of retributive justice, believing that people who murder other people should have their lives taken in return, cannot be satisfied with how the death penalty is practiced anywhere in the United States, even in those states that execute the most people. A core principle of justice is that like cases should be treated in like manner, and this is manifestly not the case with the death penalty, so no one deeply committed in principle to justice can be satisfied with our current situation.

Public opinion is deeply divided on the death penalty, though support is steadily dropping. Almost everywhere that an execution is announced, protests erupt. A disproportionate share of state resources must be devoted to every step of the death penalty process, including managing media, protests, appeals, and so on at the very end. So we could not tell our visiting alien that we execute thirty people a year here in the United States because of strong public consensus that this is the right thing to do. That is clearly not the case.

I have a theory as to why the death penalty, an anachronism from a crueler past, still survives in this vestigial form today. It requires a detour into ancient Jewish history.

The Old Testament (Hebrew Bible) contains numerous death penalty provisions. Death was prescribed as a penalty not just for murder but for a wide and surprising variety of offenses (see Exod. 21:12–17 for starters). It is interesting that the narratives of the Old Testament never actually describe an execution as prescribed in Old Testament law. But the legal texts are abundant, and they remain influential, perhaps most especially today among conservative Christians such as one finds all over the states that still execute.

But most Christians don't know that Jewish religious life did not end with the close of the canon of the Hebrew Bible. Centuries of biblical interpretation are offered in successor texts, collectively called the Talmud. Study of these texts reveals that over the centuries, the Jewish rabbis found ways to interpret the Old Testament death penalty passages so that fewer and fewer executions would actually be viewed as valid. The rabbis never simply rejected the law. They never said it was wrong for there to be death penalty provisions in the law. They just found a way to interpret the law so that it became more and more difficult to execute anyone. Somehow the combination of retaining the death penalty statutes in principle, while refusing actually to execute anyone in practice, communicated what the rabbis really wanted to say about murder. Murder is indeed a grave violation of the sacred life of the human being made in the image of God. Murder offends God and usurps God's sovereignty over human life. Murder must never be viewed as remotely acceptable or tolerable. But for a variety of reasons, the Jewish community would abstain from using execution as the punishment for murder.

It may be that, taken as a whole, the people of the United States are roughly in the same position. They want to communicate the gravity of murder. They want there to be no doubt that murder is the ultimate crime. Many want the penalty of death to remain on the books to signal these beliefs. But they want to execute people either never (in some states) or rarely (in others). This hesitation to actually apply the penalty of death flows from a variety of motives, including fears about executing an innocent person, divisions in public opinion, and a mercy/redemption strand in American culture. But the random and arbitrary pattern of executions we now have represents an offense against even the most minimal standards of justice. Real human beings randomly get taken on that long walk to the gurney, where poisons are injected into their veins by state officials representing the citizens of those states.

So here is one possible solution. Of those thirty-one states that still have the death penalty on the books, more and more could keep the statute but simply choose not to use it anymore. That is essentially what has happened in a number of states, including a large number of western states. They cannot bring themselves to abolish the penalty, but they also cannot bring themselves to use it. Perhaps it is precisely this combination that would communicate what many Americans want to see communicated in both the text of the law and its actual practice. I would go further, to the complete abolition of capital punishment. But this would be a place to start.

This issue is an example of a place where partisan politics helps us very little. Neither party has been willing to go on record in favor of banning or abandoning actual use of the death penalty. They fear the political consequences of doing so, and so the unjust status quo remains. Unless the Supreme Court intervenes, ending the death penalty will require the determined efforts of many, including Christians who are ready for this particular anachronism to leave our land, once and for all.

Chapter 19

EDUCATION

Are All Our Children Learning?

IN AN AGRARIAN ECONOMY, THE MOST IMPORTANT FORM
of capital is productive land and farm animals. In an
industrial economy, the most important form of capital is a productive factory, staffed by efficient workers.
In an information-based economy, the most important
form of capital is a good education. Most Americans
will have to make their living in the information-based
economy, or whatever comes after it. But a significant
minority of Americans are not educated adequately
for that economy. The quality of our educational system is one of the major issues all thoughtful Christians
should consider.

My wife and I raised three children. Along the way
we attempted the three major forms of education currently available in America: public schools, private

schools, and homeschooling. We learned some lessons that speak to our current national situation.

America's public schools are a massive enterprise. Controlled at the local level, with some state oversight and some federal mandates, our public schools are microcosms of the strengths and weaknesses of their local communities.

At their best, good public schools do a lot of things right. Oakton High School in Vienna, Virginia, which I attended back in the day, was an impressive school. The facilities were in very good shape, even though there were too many of us students for the space available. The teachers were generally good; the Advanced Placement teachers were so good that they were little different from college professors. Motivated students could easily launch out from Oakton High School to any of a number of high-class public and private universities. Athletic and extracurricular programs were extensive and well run. A diverse cross section of young human beings had to learn how to be together in community. For the most part they did so, contributing at least in a small way to the building of a peaceful multiracial society.

There was no particular reason why parents in Vienna, Virginia, would *need* to send their children to a private school. Of course, some did so, either for religious reasons or because they were of that pedigree that favored private schools. But the vast majority of my peers and their parents were perfectly happy with the public schools that their rather steep property taxes were paying for.

The situation was different when my children were little. We were in Jackson, Tennessee, and the public schools were not especially impressive. Facilities were often rundown. White flight to the private, mainly Christian schools had turned most public schools into underresourced, majority-black environments. Sadly, this reduced the comfort level of many white families making their school choices.

In Jackson, we sent our kids to two private Christian schools. Both were quite conservative, one of a Baptist variety and the other of the Church of Christ brand. For little kids these were nurturing, safe, loving environments suffused with a Christian ethos. At the middle school and high school levels, the religious, racial, and ideological homogeneity and conservatism of these schools was deeply problematic, and it became clearer that they were not preparing kids to live in anything other than conservative Christian subcultures within multicultural, multiracial America. Still, the overall educational quality of these Christian schools was better than that in most of the public schools; the students generally had fewer personal problems, the families were more deeply engaged, and teachers could spend the better part of each day actually teaching the assigned materials.

One semester we attempted the homeschool experience for our youngest child. Jackson was filled with homeschooling families. It was a fascinating little subculture. I saw its outcome every year when some of these kids came to college at Union University, where I was teaching. It is actually fascinating that the United States permits homeschooling, as it represents an abandonment of the part of education that involves socialization into contemporary culture with a group of peers. In my experience, most homeschool families are evangelical if not fundamentalist Christians determined to retain total control over the educational and character formation of their children through the high school years. Sometimes the students who resulted from these efforts were wonderful, sometimes they were poorly prepared for college, and sometimes they were just odd.

When we moved to Atlanta, we decided to send our children to the large public high school around the corner from our house. This school had won national awards for excellence in the 1980s. But by 2007, its better days were behind it. The facilities were acceptable. The best teachers were, again, college level. But the worst teachers were simply disastrous. The disciplinary environment at times resembled a prison, and a spirit of coercion and disrespect of students by the assistant principals was pervasive.

Of course, the problem was not just with the school. By the time students arrived in high school, they were already divided up into those who were college bound and those who were likely to drop out before junior year. "Regular" classes contained mainly the latter and far too often offered subpar educational experiences. Advanced Placement classes were excellent college-preparatory courses. In this way, the real face of the American future came into sad focus: some kids were pretty much destined for success from the cradle; others were destined to be part of that 20 percent of Americans who are unlikely to escape poverty or jail. And there was little that the high school could do, or would do, to help kids go from the second group to the first. Meanwhile, Atlanta boasted a robust private-school environment in which families with money could escape that 20 percent altogether.

If an adequate education is the primary form of capital in the information economy, those who come from families that cannot afford a private education—and often have other disadvantages—seem increasingly unlikely to get what they need from the only schools available to them. That is a massive social failure. And this is not to speak of the fact that in such an economy, a good high school education is only the beginning. College education is all the more important, and access issues are severe at this level as well.

The successful education of children requires all kinds of people rowing in the same direction. Children needs parents who love them, read to them, speak to them, invest time with them, and mold their character in the right direction. Elementary schools need teachers who love children and who supplement parental investment with the skills that they have been trained to offer. Middle and high school teachers need to know an academic area well and have the ability to design classes that educate effectively. A disciplinary environment needs to be created that is neither a prisonlike tyranny nor a "Lord of the Flies" anarchy. Facilities, equipment, and textbooks need to be adequate to their purpose. All too frequently, many of these elements are missing. Families, teachers, principals, and students are failing to do their part. And far too often, communities lack the resources or the commitment to invest adequately in their local public schools.

What is an anxious Christian to do? We need to understand that providing a quality K-12 education (and perhaps including pre-K and college) for every single person in our society is both essential to our national future and pivotal for the realization of the potential of each of these precious children of God. It is also a prudent investment; it is far better to launch someone toward professional success than to pay for their unemployment or imprisonment later. Families should think long and hard about whether to send kids to private school, asking whether that is best for them and our nation in the long run. Even in a context where we respect the separation of church and state, we need to press for a values-rich environment in all schools; educating character and casting a citizenship vision should not disappear just because the principal can't say the Lord's Prayer over the intercom. We should challenge systems of such total local control that kids from the poorest communities have to go to the nastiest schools because those schools can draw only from local property taxes. How grotesquely unfair and stupid. We can reasonably demand that every school employee be accountable and not shielded by tenure or union pro-tections from dismissal for gross incompetence. We can care. We can pay attention. We can love all our neigh-bors as ourselves.

Chapter 20

HEALTH CARE
The Unfinished Reform

HISTORY WILL RECORD THAT PRESIDENT BARACK OBAMA'S biggest domestic accomplishment was the passage of the Affordable Care Act, probably forever to be known as Obamacare. This massive and complex piece of legislation passed Congress in 2010 on straight party-line votes in both houses. Bills to kill it have been passed by the House of Representatives dozens of times since control of the House changed into Republican hands. The law may indeed be ended the next time a Republican enters the White House. Though the law is clearly flawed, I think this would be a grave mistake.

It is now clear what Obamacare does and does not do. At the time of this writing, as many as thirteen million Americans have health insurance under the ACA. A few of them are family members of mine, who are deeply appreciative of having access to health insurance and thus to at least some measure of health care. The ACA was a realistic piece of legislation in the sense that it responded to gaps in the health insurance system in our country. That system has depended on an increasingly outmoded paradigm of health insurance benefits being delivered primarily by employers. Today, however, many people work for companies that do not offer health benefits, or they are not given enough hours at work to qualify for benefits. Others are self-employed. Increasing numbers occupy a role in the service economy, such as Uber drivers or nannies. The constant churn in the job market means that even those who are fortunate enough to work full-time for an employer who provides health benefits can easily find themselves temporarily out of work or frequently shifting jobs and therefore in and out of health coverage.

As originally designed, the Affordable Care Act also made provision to plug gaps in the access of the poor to Medicaid. But Medicaid is actually delivered through the states, and some states challenged the authority of the federal government to require them to expand Medicaid access—even though all the cost at first, and most of it thereafter, was to be covered by the federal government. In the historic 2012 *National Federation of Independent Business v. Sebelius* decision on the ACA, the Supreme Court invalidated that particular requirement. As a result, many states, mainly conservative states, have chosen not to expand Medicaid access. Thus, the ACA has not had quite the reach that was envisioned in terms of expanding health insurance to many of the Americans who most need it. That is unfortunate.

Probably health care should be treated as a basic entitlement, like the right to a free K-12 education. That is how it is understood in many of our peer nations, and it makes sense. But the U.S. Constitution mainly articulates negative rather than positive rights—that is, what must not be done to us rather than what must be provided for us (at citizen expense, via taxes). Thus, health care has remained essentially a market product, delivered to those who are successful enough in the economy to be employed in a job that has health benefits for them and maybe also their families. The expansion of the social safety net that began under Franklin Roosevelt has gradually provided health coverage that is not tied to work: Medicare for senior citizens, Medicaid for the very poor, and disability insurance for those who qualify. But this has always left huge gaps, and the cost of just one serious injury or illness can destroy the financial well-being of an individual or family.

The ACA was supposed to "bend the cost curve" so that the cost of health services would become both more consistent and more reasonable. The jury is still out on whether this will actually take place. Many with adequate health coverage have no idea how much of the cost of the services we receive is waived by our providers or subsidized by our insurers. But hang out with the uninsured or the underinsured and you will find out that health care debt is one of the major factors creating misery and destroying the chance for many people to have a decent shot at financial well-being. And it must not be overlooked that even those with health insurance, including some under the ACA, have such puny benefits that they too can be driven into penury by their copayments on various expensive medicines and services. That's not health insurance worthy of the name.

So what is an anxious Christian to do about this situation? No country that was creating a health care system from scratch would come up with what we have now—a patchwork quilt of government benefits for some random bits of the population, highly diverse employment-based benefits for others, Obamacare for the working poor, and gaps for many others. The dream of a total government takeover of health care, often called a "single-payer system," seems remote, though Vermont senator and presidential candidate Bernie Sanders proposed it in the 2016 campaign. Further privatization or free-marketization of health care also seems like a denial of both the human right to receive a basic set of health care services and the cruel gaps that already exist in our health care delivery system that is tied to employment. The basic thrust of Christian advocacy on this issue should be clear: adequate, affordable, quality health care for all God's children. Every group of human beings that get covered by this or that tweak to the health care system marks a real gain for a decent society and for the reduction of human suffering.

CONCLUSION

Faithfulness and Other Strange Christian Virtues

MUCH OF THIS BRIEF SERIES OF REFLECTIONS, MY DEAR fellow Christians, has been focused on specific issues we face in America today and how Christian citizens might make a constructive contribution. Before that, I focused especially on the state of America's democracy and civic life. As I conclude, it seems timely to ask us to think together not so much about our problems and our country but about ourselves, as Christians—as the church. Who are we? Who are we called to be in this moment, in this place, right now? And where is God in all this?

The first thing to be said is that the church belongs to Jesus Christ, always and everywhere. We do not belong to any nation, nor are we a mere expression of national culture. Instead, we are a part of that international, intergenerational, intercultural community that has attempted to follow Jesus faithfully for nearly two thousand years. Our community is far older than that of any modern nation. Our ways of life, our visions of the good, our dreams for our own future and the world's future predate any nation and its ways, visions, and dreams. Our identity is in no way dependent on national identity or citizenship, and it must be protected from the excessive influence of nationality.

Especially since the rise of the modern nation-state, many Christians in many nations have given in to nationality—even to militant nationalism. The state is a great modern god; some think it is the greatest of modern gods. Gods demand and entice loyalty. Many Christians have given over loyalty to their nations in place of loyalty to Christ. Such idolatry has always been most dangerous when it is most unrecognized and most uncoerced. It is not when Caesar demands a loyalty oath that Christian fidelity is most threatened. The greatest threat is when Christians can no longer tell the difference between Caesar and Christ, prostrating themselves willingly before the former in the name of the latter.

This confusion of lords has been a perennial temptation in nations with a strong presence of Christians and with national cultures offering forms of civil religion that look and feel Christian. The old Christian nations of Europe certainly once fit that bill. And, despite constitutional disestablishment of religion, for a long time the United States offered the same temptation to Christians. We could think that ours was a Christian nation, which meant we could easily confuse loyalty to nation with loyalty to Christ. It also meant we could easily be deceived by vaguely Christian-seeming symbols and language in the public square to think that this land really was Christ's land. We so much wanted to believe it. And politicians certainly benefited from helping us believe it.

This also meant that when a growing number of Americans grew tired of Christian symbols, practices, values, beliefs, and power in their own lives or in America's life, it was probably inevitable that many Christians would respond with horror—and would organize to "take America back" for (their version of) Christian Americanism. This was the agenda of the Christian Right that mobilized in the mid-1970s. Their remnants are with us to this day, their notes struck in some form especially by any Republican running for high office. But their project has failed, and continued efforts to fan that dying ember seem more than a little pitiful.

One unexpected benefit of America's pluralization and secularization has been to reconnect the public work of the Christian church in America with an older, pre-American Christian tradition. Our Christian task looks more like it did in the earliest days of Christian faith than at any prior time in American history. We are called to live faithful Christian lives in a vast, powerful, violent, non-Christian, pluralistic, multifaith nation. The comparison of America and ancient Rome is not perfect, but it's close enough to give us something to work with as we grapple with our current situation.

There is another danger associated with our current moment that must be named as well. It is especially a temptation for those who reject the conservative "Take

America back for Christ" project. This danger is that some Christians in America will become too comfortable here, gradually becoming unable to tell the difference between the way of life appropriate to those who are committed to Jesus Christ and the way of life of American majority culture. Of course, there have always been gaping holes between Christ's way and "the American way," among them our terrible systemic evil in relation to race. At various points in this book I have sought gently but clearly to name this and other patterns of living that are not a fit with the way of life taught by Christ and more broadly in the Bible. These have included unfettered selfishness in commerce; routine resort to war; arbitrary and discriminatory criminal-justice practices; casual sex, marriage, and divorce; consumption of degrading media; and routine resort to abortion.

Just as Christian faithfulness does not mean seeking a restoration of Christian America, it also does not mean obscuring the difference between Christ's way and other ways. But culture is a powerful thing, and in recent decades the very plausibility of many historic Christian moral convictions has seemed to collapse, even among Christians. It is easy to move into a "go along to get along" mentality in a culture whose values clash with Christian beliefs. But as with Christian nationalism, the danger is much more severe when we have no idea we are surrendering important ground to sub-Christian cultural practices. I am thinking of all kinds of things here, including Christian acceptance of materialism, drug use, pornography, violence, casual sex, and obscene language. Sometimes it seems that

Christians today consider it a badge of honor to be as indistinguishable from our neighbors as possible on matters such as these.

For future generations of Christians to be able to tell the difference between our ways and alien ways, between who we are and who we must not be, the church must survive as a body with biblical seriousness, historical memory, and cultural sensitivity without surrender. Churches must retain the capacity to teach Christian faithfulness into the teeth of a sometimes hostile culture—without anger, without panic, but also without confusion.

This is not a problem only on the political left or the political right. Cultural currents that violate the moral structure of Christian faith can come from any direction. They can be right-wing nativism or militarism, or left-wing libertinism or statism, or culture-wide indifference to prisoners and the poor. This means that no part of the Christian community can relax about the dangers of moral surrender, even though surrender takes so many different forms.

I have implied that retaining practiced faithfulness to the way of Jesus Christ is the core challenge for Christians in America, as in any nation-state. I have not said that directly until now, but I have intended that it should undergird everything in this book.

Of course, ours is a massive and contested tradition. There is hardly total agreement in the churches about the actual moral demands of Christian faithfulness. But there is a long and ongoing conversation available to each of us as we seek to discern what faithfulness requires. At the very least, America's Christians (like all other Christians) need to develop their way(s) of life in dialogue with that historic, explicitly Christian moral tradition—rather than having such a thin Christian identity that we are really being fundamentally formed by other visions of the good life. Our scholars, ministers, and other leaders bear the greatest responsibility to initiate Christians into this body of Christian moral tradition. Too often we fail, even when Christians are in church looking for guidance.

There is one final set of questions I think we need to consider before this "letter" ends. Where is God in all of this? What is God doing right now in our land? Or has God gone away in search of a people more interested in God's will?

The easy answer, at least to the last question, is that God already has a people. Christians call that people the church. (And we are not the only ones who consider ourselves *the* or *a* people of God.) With the exception of biblical Israel, Christian theology does not recognize any national community as the people of God. But Christians in practice, at least in the Christendom era running from Constantine forward, have often been tempted to identify their own national community as God's elect, as God's most favored nation. It is a habit of mind that easily flows from immersion in the Old Testament texts of chosen peoplehood, often in combination with a Christian assumption that God has replaced Israel with another chosen people. The New Testament often identifies chosen peoplehood with the church (1 Pet. 2:9). It never identifies any national group as God's new chosen people. But Christians have often been tempted to do just that.

So it is not constructive to suggest that America was once God's elect and is no more or that it could again be God's chosen if we would just repent and turn back to God. But still the question remains: where is God among us right now?

I believe that we can be fully confident that our sovereign God, who loved the world so much that he sent his only Son (John 3:16), is actively engaged within the borders of this nation each day—just like everywhere else. I believe that God is, here as everywhere, calling those who claim to be God's people to live out the moral demands of their faith. I believe that Jesus made it clear that the moral demands of the faith he taught centered on love, justice, and mercy (Matt. 22:36–40; 23:23). I believe that God is, here as everywhere, nudging Christians and all other human beings toward love—love for the Creator, love for other people, love for self, love for the world God has made.

I do not believe that God has a special plan for American preeminence. I do not believe that God can be counted on to do miracles to preserve our carefully designed democracy from our own mistakes, just as I do not believe God will rescue humanity from the ecological degradations we are visiting on creation. We are responsible for the decisions we are making, and we will not be shielded from their consequences. I believe in a God who teaches human beings the right way—individually and collectively—and then invites us, in freedom, to live it out. This is why I am asking you to attend very closely both to the health of our democratic institutions and the structure of our national policies. American Christian political responsibility involves navigations at a four-way intersection: deep historic Christian moral commitments, specific national challenges today, our particular constitutional democracy, and a swiftly changing culture. Within this crowded intersection, we seek to discern what faithfulness requires.

If some of our worst anxieties turn out to be well founded—if we elect horrendous leaders, if we allow our democracy to erode into a banana republic, if we cannot solve our social and policy problems—it will, of course, really matter. It will mark a huge loss for America, for those who live here, for all who are affected by what our country does. But even if any or all of this happens, God will still be God, and the church will still be the church. We will wake up with the same basic obligations that we had the day before, but in a much more challenging environment.

So, fellow Christians, do not give in to fear. Be determined, not anxious. Live in faithfulness to Jesus Christ, come what may, among these neighbors we are called to love, in this land that is our home.